The
DREAMLIFE
of JOHNNY
BASEBALL

The
DREAMLIFE
of JOHNNY
BASEBALL

edited by

RICHARD
GROSSINGER

North Atlantic Books
Berkeley, California

The Dreamlife of Johnny Baseball

ISBN 1-55643-003-5 (cloth)
ISBN 1-55643-002-7 (paperback)

Published by North Atlantic Books
            2320 Blake Street
            Berkeley, California 94704

Cover painting by Tom Clark
Title page art by Thom Ross
Cover and book design by Paula Morrison
Typeset in Bookman by Classic Typography
This is #40 in the *Io* series.

This project is partially supported by grants from the National Endowment for the Arts, a Federal agency, and the California Arts Council,
an agency of the State of California.

The Dreamlife of Johnny Baseball is sponsored by the Society for
the Study of Native Arts and Sciences, a nonprofit educational corpor-
ation whose goals are to develop an ecological and crosscultural perspec-
tive linking various scientific, social, and artistic fields; to nurture a
holistic view of arts, sciences, humanities, and healing; and to publish
and distribute literature on the relationship of mind, body, and nature.

Library of Congress Cataloging in Publication Data

The Dreamlife of Johnny Baseball.

   (Io ; no. 40)
   1. Baseball—United States.   I. Grossinger, Richard,
1944–   . II. Series.
GV863.A1D74 1987   796.357'64'0973   87-13987
ISBN 1-55643-003-5
ISBN 1-55643-002-7 (pbk.)

CONTENTS

Richard Grossinger

NOTES ON THE 1986 PLAYOFFS AND WORLD SERIES

> *"It's a bit hard to realize that, the only time you were a real poet in your life was when you were only 25-years old, sprawled out in right-center field at Shea Stadium, praying that you'd catch a line drive off Brooks Robinson's bat. In everything I've done in my life since then, I've tried to recapture that feeling, that sense of true poetry. But perhaps it only happens once."* Ron Swoboda.

Jesse Orosco heaves his glove into the night sky and kneels on the mound in a jubilation that is also spontaneous prayer. He is burning an indelible moment onto thousands of highlight films that will proceed into the future cloning one another until no one will remember how we got to it or feel any longer the emotions of two embattled teams. Its future is to become stale newsreel iconography. But its present moment is like a hot log crashing to the ground, releasing thousands of embers, flashbacks in baseball time. No amount of replays or recalls can ever bring that phenomenom back.

The most recent of the embers is barely hours old: Trailing 3-0, the Mets went down quietly in the bottom of the fifth inning in their twenty-second shot at an insoluble Bruce Hurst. "Is it for real this time, or are we being led on again?" I asked my friend Nick with feigned optimism.

"I am *sure* we are being led on," he said.

At that moment I had little hope; it seemed the Mets' miracle sixth-game comebacks had merely postponed an inevitable

Boston victory (made inevitable by Dave Henderson's destiny-changing home run in the fifth game of the American League playoffs). Then suddenly, sparked for the second straight night by a Lee Mazzili pinch single, New York rallied to tie the score; an inning later they took the lead. The bottom of the sixth began a charge to the end of the season reminiscent only (among "seventh games") of the back-and-forth reversals of the Yankees-Pirates finale in 1960. For a brief duration the Mets and the Red Sox each seemed to have the momentum to overcome whatever the other did. Against Roger McDowell, who mowed them down an inning before, the Sox rallied for two runs on three hits in the top of the eighth and had the tying run on second with no one out when Orosco entered the game—shades of Dale Long and Mickey Mantle in the bottom of the ninth in Pittsburgh. But suddenly the revels ended; the 1986 post-season goblin had played his last trick.

Most baseball games are simply ordinary; even with a few remarkable moments, most seasons in a team's history are humdrum and equalizing. For a franchise only twenty-five years old, however, the Mets have found themselves in a couple of centuries worth of both bizarre games and unlikely seasons. Before the 1986 playoffs even began, they could supply a full resume of marathons—25 innings against the Cardinals in 1974, 24 against the Astros in 1968 (ending 1–0), 23 against the Giants in the second game of a doubleheader in 1964 (they lost all three).* Other Met sagas played right into "The Twilight Zone." For instance, in their 19-inning battle in Atlanta in '85 the Mets tied the score against Bruce Sutter in the ninth; they took the lead twice in extra innings only to have the Braves retie it each time on home runs. The second such homer, with two outs in the seventeenth, was hit by pitcher Rick Camp (because the Braves had run out of pinch-hitters). Camp came to the plate with virtually no chance even of getting a hit let alone hitting a home run; he had one of

---

*Bob Ojeda, the first Met pitcher to win a post-season game since Jerry Koosman in 1973, worked the top of the 33rd inning for Pawtucket in 1981 and was the winning pitcher in the longest game in professional baseball history. He was a *Red Sox* farmhand at the time—an obvious Met in training.

the worst batting averages in the history of baseball. (Are we being led on . . . indeed?) (It seemed almost part of the bewitching that Tom Gorman, the victim of both home runs, thought he was pitching to Gene Garber at the time.) The Mets did finally win, 16–13, but not before Camp came to the plate again as the tying run and made the final out.

The Mets' 1962 season was a classic of blown ballgames and unlucky losses defying the law of averages. Then in 1969, against 100–1 odds, the Mets won the first Eastern Division Championship of the National League in a charmed late-season run that included a doubleheader of 1–0 wins over Pittsburgh (with the pitcher driving in the only run in both games) and a victory over Steve Carlton in which 19 Mets struck out but Ron Swoboda hit two two-run homers. Players like Wayne Garrett and Al Weis then rose from ordinary careers to get clutch hits off all-star pitchers and lead the team to the Pennant and the World Championship.

In 1973, behind Tug McGraw, the Mets came from under .500 and just out of last place in September to win the Division. In one improbable game they outlasted the Expos (who repeatedly loaded the bases with less than two outs in extra innings); they rallied from two runs down in the ninth inning against Dave Giusti and the Pirates, winning on a single by Ron Hodges; they beat the Pirates two days later on an extra-inning "non-home-run" that bounced off the railing into Cleon Jones' glove (Dave Augustine was thrown out trying for it inside-the-park). They then survived the Big Red Machine in an intense five-game play-off and, on the heels of a Koosman gem, took a 3–2 lead in the World Series out to Oakland. But it was not until thirteen years later that the franchise won its next Series game—at Fenway, behind Ojeda too.

Although they hit the doldrums between 1974 and 1983, the Mets still managed singular masterpieces (for example, Mookie Wilson's dramatic two-run ninth-inning homer off Bruce Sutter of the Cardinals after the 1981 strike, Terry Leach's ten-inning one-hitter over the Phillies in 1983). When they emerged again as a contender, it was straight up out of last place, as it had been in '69. In '84 and '85, the Mets were the bare loser in two gripping races culminating in pivotal September series, first with the Cubs, then with the Cardinals; at the same time they unveiled the most sudden and dominating phenom pitcher of recent memory, Dwight Gooden.

By 1986 everything seemed to have changed, including the Mets' historic status as beloved underdog: From the beginning of the season they were everybody's favorites to win the Eastern Division, and then went wire to wire virtually unchallenged. They replaced the Yankees as the hated media-center team. Seeking to scapegoat someone in the role of the arrogant front-runner, fans focussed on the public personae of Ray Knight and Gary Carter, the high emotion the Mets displayed on the field, plus a few provoked fights, and exaggerated these into a cartoon bully.

But the Mets' fire of '86 was less arrogance than a carry-over of the draining losses of '84 and '85. They maintained a contact electricity with the fans at Shea, to whom they in essence made a promise when they came back onto the field after the last home games of those seasons and tossed their caps into the stands—not necessarily to win but to keep the dream alive. The Mets are still more notable for their humane treatment of minor-league players, using the farm system as a school; their graciousness about players traded to other organizations (wishing them well as 'always Mets'); their repayment of the loyalty of Rick Anderson, Ed Hearn, Terry Leach, and others; and their low-key and entirely professional public profile in New York.

Although the 1986 Mets reached the playoffs as if they were an imposter, the team that parried the Astros and Red Sox was basically the same group that was intimidated by Chicago Cubs in '84 and that battled the flashy and egotistic Cardinals down to a single game in '85; they had little to do with the New York Yankees or any other legendary New York team. They were pure Met, and by the time '86 was over, fans were still not sure what they had seen.

Of course, the Red Sox are another team with a textured and complicated history of improbable games and seasons. Many a Boston fan considered their own team legitimately the one with soul, the Mets another New York ogre—a sign at Fenway during the third game expressed the mood well: Red Sox 2, Mets 0; Yankees: No Game Today. (An intellectual left-wing graduate student, who had been a generally restrained, pro-Mets Red Sox fan, surprised me after the Series by saying that he now considered the Mets an obnoxious, arrogant team. It was a tough loss, I sympathized, but the Mets weren't showing off, they were just happy, and relieved. *I* had thought some of the Red Sox arrogant: Remember Roger Clemens yukking it up when he thought the sixth game was on ice. I mean it wasn't Gary Carter who voted himself MVP and then called Henry Aaron a publicity hound for saying he preferred an everyday player like Don Mattingly.)

The World Series brought together two zany legends that finally played themselves out to the limit in games six and seven.

Do teams have their own individual myth cycles? The notion seems romantic and farfetched at first glance; certainly players vehemently deny any jinx from earlier seasons (especially ones played before they were on the team, or, in some cases, even born). Yet, there are curious recurrences: the Red Sox of the supposed "Harry Frazee" curse are the franchise that sold Babe Ruth and other stars to the Yankees (creating the great American League dynasty of the 1920's and '30's if not of all time); they are the team that was paralyzed by Enos Slaughter's inspired dash in the eighth inning of the seventh game in 1946, that lost the seventh game to the Cardinals again, behind Bob Gibson in '67, that blew a one-game lead to the Yankees with two games left in '49 (giving Casey Stengel his first pennant and initiating an incredible string of World Series appearances over the next sixteen years), that was turned back again in the seventh game of the '75 Series by Tony Perez, Pete Rose, and the Reds *immediately after* their own miraculous sixth-game win (New England's entry for the greatest game ever played); and then they were the victims of the Yankees' late-season dash of 1978 culminating in the unlikely Bucky Dent home run in the one-game playoff (New England's singlemost game of infamy).

The Yankees have their own distinctive Ugly American/ carpetbagger heritage (their very name resounds through Latin America in "Yanquis Go Home"); the legacy is so deliberate and conscious that George Steinbrenner was able to resurrect it merely by buying the franchise and then Catfish Hunter and Reggie Jackson (just as Babe Ruth, Lou Gehrig, Joe Dimaggio, Mickey Mantle, and Yogi Berra were purchased before them—I mean these guys weren't draft picks). The Cubs have a sentimental downbeat tradition, from early World Series folds, to the fade of '69, to Leon Durham's error in the '84 playoffs—highlighting the collapse of what seemed an unstoppable pennant surge at Wrigley just days earlier. (How did Sutcliffe, Dernier, and company all turn into pumpkins at precisely the bewitching hour?)

The Cardinals of 1984, with Willie McGee and Vince Coleman, were a true Gashouse Gang throwback, streamlined and funked up for the '80s. The Dodgers of Valenzuela and company recall the interregnum of Drysdale and Koufax who recall the Brooklyn duo of Erskine and Labine. (On the other hand, teams like the Pirates and Phillies of the '70s seem quantum breaks in the tradition of their franchises.)

The 1986 post-season played itself out within the established destinies of the teams involved. The Angels blew the big game, and then self-destructed. It was an all-time frustrating miss for a franchise whose most heroic identity remains the expansion team of Ken McBride, Leon Wagner, and George and LeRoy Thomas.

The Red Sox saw the ghosts of 1946, 1949, 1967, 1975, and 1978. How often can you miss from *that* close?

The Astros enacted their own unique tradition with exquisite precision. From the time they were born simultaneously with the New York Mets in 1962 (as the Houston Colt .45s), they have been locked in a transcendantal pitching duel with their twin, supplying the likes of Dick Farrell and Mike Cuellar, Don Wilson and Larry Dierker, James Rodney Richard and Bob Knepper (remember the historic 24-inning 1–0 game at the Astrodome). These two teams are headed toward a fifty inning scoreless tie before the end of this century. The Mets were at a definite disadvantage until the era of Seaver, Koosman, and Gentry, reenacted now by Gooden, Darling, and company. (Ironically enough, the two most dominating pitchers on the '86 Astros were ex-Mets Mike Scott and Nolan Ryan. In three of the six playoff games they were all but unhittable.)

Insofar as the 1986 National League Championship Series was enacted by two teams locked in a millennial pitching duel, single, almost incidental plays took on ultracritical significance. The Met Pennant was the result only of a conspiracy of infinitesimal episodes, any *one* of which going the other way could have tilted the series to the Astros.

How tight were the playoffs? The winning team, the Mets, entered 29 of the 64 innings tied, another 29 behind, and only 6 ahead. All of those 6 were in the second game! They never entered an inning ahead during the three games at their home ballpark yet won two of them!

How many times do we hear that a team is presently 40–1 or 85–2 when they hold the lead going into the ninth inning? Yet three times in twelve *regular-season* games the Astros were tied by the Mets in the ninth or tenth (though they recovered to win the last two of those in Houston). Darryl Strawberry's ninth-inning homer off Dave Smith tying the eleventh game of the regular season between the two teams was exactly prescient of Len Dykstra's dramatic home run off Smith turning defeat into victory in the third game of the playoffs. At the time that was the most intense game of the season, but when the World Series had run its weird course, it seemed more like an intimation.

Home runs by Strawberry and Knight respectively tied and then won a July game in the tenth inning at Shea—much in the fateful way the Mets would come from behind late in the third and sixth games of the playoffs. In the fifth playoff game only one well-timed swing by Darryl Strawberry prevented Nolan Ryan from shutting the Mets out and sending the series back to Houston with the Astros ahead. That homer kept New York in the game until Gary Carter could punch his tension-breaking grounder through Charlie Kerfeld's legs in the twelfth. [My teenage son Robin, a lifelong Met fan, had elected to go to French class with a transistor and an earphone (no one else in his Oakland school was that involved in the game). I had told him he could stay home, but he considered his act a nostalgic throwback to my tales of radios and daytime World Series from childhood and he wanted to experience that ancient feeling for himself. As he recounted it: "When Carter got the hit, I let out a whoop. It really shook up the teacher. When she found out why, she threatened to take away the radio; at least I think that's what *appareil* means".] (Meanwhile, detractors of Strawberry's post-season play tend to overlook not only that home run off Ryan but the three-run shot that tied Knepper in the Dykstra game and then the solo homer off Al Nipper that clinched the seventh game of the World Series. Strawberry could have struck out every single other at bat—and almost did—and still have had one of the great clutch post-seasons of all time. His first two homers were game-transforming shots off pitchers in absolute grooves.)

As unusual as the '86 playoffs were, the Astros must have had the feeling they had been there before. For Mike Schmidt, it was deja vû 1980, fourth and fifth games (under the old five-game format). The Phillies won the first game of that series at home and almost took the second too: As Astro pitcher Frank LaCorte walked dejectedly off the mound, Bake McBride, carrying the winning run, was inexplicably held at third by coach Lee Elia. Houston eventually won, setting the stage for everything that would follow.

The Astros also took the third game, typically 1–0 in 11 innings, and, when they carried a 2–0 lead forged against Steve Carleton into the eighth inning at the Dome, it looked like curtains for the Phillies.

No! The Phils scored three runs to take the lead; then the Astros countered with one in the ninth to send the game into extra innings. In the tenth, pinch-hitter Greg Luzinski doubled to left, and Pete Rose scored all the way from first with a forearm to Bruce Bochy's face.

The next day the Phillies found themselves in an even worse position—down 5–2 going into the eighth inning against Nolan Ryan in his prime. Then, keyed by Del Unser's critical pinch hit, they exploded for five runs; the Astros miraculously answered with two in the bottom of the inning. In the tenth, Gary Maddox doubled in Unser with the Pennant-winner.

After watching the Mets and Astros carry their monumental battle into extra innings (and evening) at the Astrodome, Schmidt recalled the desperation of the 1980 Phillies on "New York Sports Nightly." To paraphrase him from memory: "It was the Astrodome, where they believed they were unbeatable; it was Nolan Ryan; they had us by three runs; we had two shots left; there was no way they could lose. Same thing today; only it was Bob Knepper and he had the Mets beat through eight innings. Yes, the Mets won it, but the Astros once again lacked something extra needed to close it out."

Dramatic turnaround at the point of victory (or defeat) was the hallmark of the 1986 post-season, with only the Mets surviving. (It actually began with the Kansas City Royals' stunning reversals over the Blue Jays and Cardinals in 1985. The sixth game of the 1985 World Series was the only time all season the Cardinals' bullpen blew a lead in the last inning.) How many times during the regular season does a good team carry a *two-* or *three-* run lead into the last inning, and lose? Yet it happened four times in twenty post-season games in 1986, including twice with two out. Perhaps these post-season dramatics reflect a level of intensity missing during the regular season. Players enter an almost psychic state, pushing their abilities to the limit to try individually to wrest the outcome. Some players anyway. . . . Or maybe an undiagnosed archetype prevails.

Let's review that epic ninth-inning rally in Houston: The Mets had gone down meekly that afternoon without even threatening for eight innings (and for essentially the preceding twenty-one in New York); they opened the ninth with Lenny Dykstra, a lefthanded pinch-hitter (because there were no viable right-handed ones left) against a dominating left-handed pitcher. Dykstra drove a triple to right center field. Perhaps Billy Hatcher should have caught it, but he certainly wasn't playing Dykstra to pull Knepper. Billy Doran *could* have caught Mookie Wilson's soft liner if he had judged his leap properly. When Hernandez hit a shot to center one out later, the tying run was on second. Dave Smith came in again and painstakingly walked both Carter and Strawberry; now the flow of energy had turned in the Mets' direction. Ray Knight's ensuing at-bat was the key. First, Knight almost walked, and was furious at the umpire's call; then he almost struck out. When Astro catcher Alan Ashby challenged this second call, Knight turned and started yelling at *him*. It was no more big salaries, primetime showbiz bullshit; these guys were playing hardball. Knight muscled a shot deep enough to right to bring in Hernandez. Danny Heep could have ended it all by taking four balls, but he fidgeted through customary half swings and struck out.

Now the game marched off into never-never land, freezing baseball fans in a trance for almost the duration of a second entire sudden-death game. Robin followed it on and off much of the day at school, on the car radio driving home, and then came crashing in the door wide-eyed during the eleventh. "This is amazing!" he said. It was. It was one game for which I had no precedent. It was the whole of what baseball is, all at once. Its background intensity—from game to game, season to season—had come forward into an actual event and taken over an entire day.

When Wally Backman singled home a run in the fourteenth inning, a Met Pennant was almost tastable. We hung before the TV, waiting. Orosco struck out Billy Doran to open the bottom of the inning. But suddenly and without forewarning, Billy Hatcher hit a tremendous home run just fair down the leftfield line. There was no way out of this game. Exhausted players were on the roller-coaster and they had to ride it to the end.

Like in the marathon against the Braves the Mets were engaged in a life-and-death struggle, but this time for their whole season. Although Keith Hernandez confided to a number of Astros on the basepaths, "Isn't this a great game," there was no way for the teams to declare it a tie, shake hands, and walk off the field. The ancient ballcourt had two different exits, and eventually everyone on that field, and every fan following the two teams, would take one or the other. Yet it *was* a collaboration, and the teams honored each other merely by being in it together. The Astros, by providing a worthy foe, made the Mets' season heroic (they also exhausted them to such a degree that they sleepwalked through the first two games of the World Series).

The way Houston (and Mike Scott) finished the season, the Mets were walking open-eyed into a buzzsaw. The Astros should have been heavy betting favorites over even the '27 Yankees. By making it through the buzzsaw, the Mets defined themselves as a team. Then a softer version of the same curious puzzle was thrown at them in the Series (with Bruce Hurst replacing Mike Scott), and in surviving that, they completed a mythic season.

When the Mets went to the well for the Pennant against the Astros in the extra innings of that sixth game, I was transfixed in the tension; their whole team history passed before me. It was such a sinuous many-season path to this climax that the ordinary events of a baseball game couldn't express the emotions of it. The real energy of the hour existed in an aura that surrounded the game, perceptible only to those who followed it at that level. Otherwise, it was just a bunch of men playing baseball on television, or, to the incidental fan, at best a crucial playoff game.

(George Leonard refers accurately to the aikido black belt exam, or the World Series game "during which every last spectator realizes at some level that what is happening out on the field is more than a game, but rather something achingly beautiful and inevitable, an enactment in space and time of how the universe works, how things are.")

To the fan of a team, such a game is a hologram reflecting the hundreds of other games which pass through it. Seasons upon seasons are played in order to come to moments like these; so when you participate in the millennial game, you are reliving the memory of those seasons, the subtle textures of their innings and players.

Likewise, the true follower watches the prior seasons of eliminated teams through the imagined crystal of this famous moment (whether it happens or not), for it is the potential of winning the Pennant and Series that gives each season its taut boundaries and keeps the games meaningful. As in any ceremony, the significators are hidden and the deep image is concealed in the simple event sequence on the surface. A game this big cannot contain itself.

Thus, Jesse Orosco pitching for the Mets at the moment of truth was also the Jesse Orosco of 1979 and 1982, who failed as a rookie after coming over in a trade for Jerry Koosman, who worked his way back through the minors and then ran off a marvellous skein of saves and wins in 1983. It was the same Jesse Orosco who gave several up game-tying and winning home runs over the years, but who also regularly got the game-ending strikeout with the tying or winning runs on base. He would never again be as good as he was in '83, but by the time he took the mound in Houston he had a complex history, he had individuated—and, in the end, he was good enough. Mike Scott may have been better, but the game wasn't in Mike Scott's hands. Jesse Orosco in the Astrodome (and in the ninth inning of the seventh Series game at Shea) was also John Pacella and Scott Holman. All of those images of pitchers on the mound in Met uniforms flow together. Likewise, hundreds of shadow Wally Backmans and Mookie Wilsons combine in memory to frame the single narrative stream of an afternoon. Only to the incidental fan will Mookie be wed to the grounder that eluded Bill Buckner to end the sixth Series game. To the Met fan he will always be scoring from second on a groundout, running down alley shots, and slashing lightning homers inside either foul pole.

The Mets were not born contending in 1984; they do not take their identity from only the successful season of 1986. All of the players who didn't make it to Houston are still present. Steve Henderson and Hubie Brooks are there; how could Hubie not be a part of it? Though long gone, Henderson struck a franchise-changing three-run homer off the Giants' Alan Ripley to win a lone game one June in New York. Recalled from exile, Lee Mazzili represents Doug Flynn and Frank Taveras. But also everyone else participates, from Leon Brown to Craig Swan, from Charlie Puleo to young erratic Mike Scott and Jeff Reardon. If they weren't there, it wouldn't be the Mets; it would just be some good team winning the Pennant, the same thing some good team does every year. Most of all, John Stearns is there, kneeling in the dust by home plate, his fist clenched while runs pour across, never losing the fire or dignity. That image was waiting five, eight years, to be redeemed in this game. No matter how physical these games are, their real truth lies in the spirits not the bodies of those that play. (Do you doubt that if the New Jersey Nets ever win the championship, however many decades in the future, Buck Williams will be there rebounding . . . for all his leaps from beyond exhaustion in the fourth quarter, for all the hopeless games and meaningless seasons in which he refused to give up?)

I think you must look inward because "inside" is where it's coming from; otherwise, what would the game mean but tin soldiers on a toy field, or data pouring through computer terminals? Yes, we are in an era of "acting out" and externalities, from jihads and nuclear bombs to heavy metal, venture capital, and quick sex, but it is the human experience of those things that gives them texture and power over us. Throughout those extra innings I kept asking myself—Why? Why does this (which means nothing at all) mean so much I can barely breathe?

Familiar insights replayed themselves—the joy of collective participation with all the other people identifying with the Mets . . . projection of my psyche into a certified mythic event . . . transference of my paralyzed sympathy for everyone to just these players (because they are particularized and universal, as I wrote in *The Temple of Baseball*). I think of the Mets as standing for all the black kids in Berkeley schoolyards wearing blue NY caps for the first time, the guys in motorized wheelchairs with Mets bumperstickers, plus the various people, Met fans or not, with whom I have shared my insights into the team.

Other thoughts come less easily: I experience that I am fragmented and contracted, never a whole coherent organism. The part of me that is locked into the game is isolated from the real hungers and desires of the self, so it thrives off the exercise of strong emotion bound in this event. Not capable somehow of the full tenderness of the life itself, "I" prefer some hit from outside that's at least also real, i.e., not a story or a fantasy. (The reason it can't be movie stars or rock singers is that they win every time, whatever they do; their mere persona is a display of triumph.) The advantage of the game is that its unfolding occurs apart from anything I can intervene to change, like geology or astronomy—which is why rotisserie leagues seem sterile to me: who cares about imposing the aggrandizing manipulative self on an event that has its own integrity.

Watching myself watch the game is like the meditation required of life itself. You are bound to watch it. Although it's not real in the way it seems to be real, you are also called upon to participate in it on the deepest possible level. The game is a test for life, which is even more in doubt than it, and which we likewise enter from a long history (biological and cultural) that gives it meaning. (Sometimes, in thinking of death, one of the things I find it hardest to imagine is that the Mets will go on playing games the results of which I will never know with players I have never heard of.)

But I don't want to dwell on metaphors and symbols. My participation in the Mets is finally unconscious, or semi-conscious at best, and only secondarily intellectual. During the playoffs my wife Lindy remarked that the intensity of me and my son were absurd to her. "Who cares?" she said. "This doesn't affect or interest me, and it's an intrusion on my life." One night she added in exasperation: "I don't get it. Are we involved in professional baseball? I didn't get married to have professional baseball imposed on me." I was mortified; it *did* look ridiculous. (Later I told Tom Clark, the poet, and he said, "Tell her it could be worse; you could be involved in college baseball.")

Put under the gun by her as much as myself, I couldn't just

watch passively. At least if I was going to be there, I needed to answer some of the questions. Given the world situation, given the existential life situation, how important could this game be?

But baseball is not only a practice of life; it is a practice of practice, and we have to probe it not for the obvious symbols baseball philosophers are fond of pointing out in the American frontier psyche but for the nature of our attachment to those symbols.

Then, in the extreme condition of the extra innings against Houston, I perceived a new level: It's not just that baseball involves a fragment of my personality. It's that the game brings together two fragmented selves I spend much of my life trying to meld on an unconscious level. There is the positive visionary self, that writes, that seeks spiritual discipline, that communicates from the heart not the mind, that is capable of unquestioning love. The part of me who has not atained this level but is addicted to its poignancy tries to get a "rush" out of the game. Real transformation doesn't happen, but at the moment it doesn't matter, the semblance of it does. Just because it's baseball is no reason to trash it; we little enough understand the sources and accessibility of the tremendous energy we each contain.

At the same time, there exists the dreading anxious part of me, the self that is overwhelmed by the danger of the streets, the threat of nuclear war, the ever nearness of disaster and loss. That being has occupied as much of my inner life as the visionary. Its basic style is to move from one dread to another, to be satisfied only when some imagined catastrophe doesn't happen—the hysteria of continually postponed air raid sirens.

The "sudden death" of the sixth playoff game is an opportunity for both selves. Each time the Astros come up I "practice" my anxiety and observe it. Each time the Mets come up I yearn for my visionary high in the form of the Pennant. I go back and forth between the two and experience their nearness. And I realize that it has always been this way. The two intensities are the polar boundaries of my emotional life and the game allows me to project them and enjoy their pure oscillations without dilution or distraction. However I get there, this deeply charged state is crucial to me.

For Robin it is not quite the same. He enjoys the mere fact the Mets are in this game, and though he will be depressed and teary if they lose, he is not negative during it. In fact, I drive him crazy through the eleventh, the twelfth, thirteenth, fourteenth innings, kicking the ground, drumming with my leg, hitting the chair every time a pitch doesn't go right. I am unconscious of these gestures, but he tells me, so I leave the garage and go to the TV inside where my twelve-year-old daughter Miranda is reading a book and cares only insofar that if the Mets win, I have promised a walk to the bakery for a victory cake.

When the Knight singles in Strawberry in the top of the sixteenth, I go back outside for the rest of the three-run rally, but I flee when the Astros begin scoring in the bottom half. Robin and I are simply too much for each other right now. The game is the epitome of no control, with the history of baseball at stake: The Astros are within one hit of an all-time miracle comeback recalling Bobbie Thomson's home run, and I can do nothing but pace in stunned silence.

Later we learn that, at that dangerous moment, Keith Hernandez came to the mound and jokingly told Carter, "No more fast balls, or you'll have to fight me right here." (Carter later denied this and attributed it to Hernandez's buoyant postgame mood when he talked fast and loose, as one is inclined to in the giddiness of such a time. When reality has transcended myth, it has become myth, and one is tempted to create an archetypal version of what happened because it alone seems true.) But the point is: Hernandez is thinking all the time about the game situation (the same mind used on Civil War battles and crosword puzzles). He is never paralyzed. There are very few players who are so alert to the nuances, who are so present in the game that they become the game, and enact profound baseball logic without thinking. Hernandez is the baseball equivalent of an aikido master. His intelligence does not require self-consciousness. That's why he went to second to nip Hatcher on Walling's grounder in the hole that inning. If he had taken the easier play at first— which is what most infielders in the history of the game would have done—Glenn Davis' ensuing single would have tied the score (. . . another of those intricate subsets of possibility that propelled the Mets rather than the Astros into the World Series!).

In another sense, that "game intelligence"* is why Her-

---

*Even certain hits have far more mind than body in them, though the exclusivity of the terms finally breaks down.

nandez got the key ninth-inning double off Knepper after not hitting him all day; it's also why he was the one who broke the ice off Bruce Hurst in the seventh game of the Series with a bases-loaded single, precisely the deed he performed for the Cardinals against the Brewers, seventh game, 1982—essentially the identical hit (off another difficult lefty, Bob McClure). ("We don't change," the poet said; "we merely stand revealed.") When games and whole seasons come down to infinitesimal points, it is these bits of disciplined mentality on which the result turns. Of course, Hernandez would perceive all curve balls to Kevin Bass (Bass would finally swing and miss strike three—pandemonium, release at last from this game!). Like in chess, the strategy unfolds until a weakness is revealed: the lefthanded side of the Astros' bullpen, the Red Sox pitching after Clemens and Hurst. Not always, but enough for confirmation.

After the game, Mike Schmidt's first observation was about Bass. "Only by failing in that situation," he said, "do you learn how to succeed the next time. When you succeed, it's not some out-of-the blue thing. You reach back inside yourself into the prvious failure and that's the place you succeed from." He was telling us a secret. When he struck out with the tying run on third in the fifth game of the 1980 playoffs, that was the spot from which hundreds of clutch hits would later come.

The Mets started the World Series the same way they started the playoffs, losing 1–0, although in a lower-energy game, decided not by a home run but a ground ball through Tim Teufel's legs. They lost the second game, too, when Dwight Gooden was soundly thumped. The forces at large seemed profoundly opposed to a Met victory; in the fourth inning, tremendous shots to right field by both Strawberry and Howard Johnson simply died against a cushion of air. It was as though the Sox were swinging against the moon's gravity, the Mets against Neptune's.

To many observers, including ones who had predicted a Met sweep, it was all over. But not to Mike Schmidt, nor the Astros. "We were both depleted after that series," said a Houston coach, "we drained each other. The Mets expected to breeze after us, so they're running on empty, but they'll wake up."

Schmidt said that if he were the manager, he would tell the players, "All you have to do is win two in a row. How many times have you done that this year? Forty times maybe."

The Mets went up to Boston and did precisely that. They didn't even wait for a chance to fall behind again. As the first batter in game three, Len Dykstra, a self-activating spark, stroked a home run ("Did you see where he hit one the last series of the year in Philly against us," reminded Schmidt); then, the Mets scorched Oil Can Boyd for three more first-inning runs, and, though he held them off from there till the seventh, it was enough.

The following day Gary Carter found a leftfield screen clearly made for his stroke, twice. The Green Monster, like the wind at Shea, became the ally of the visitors (Mookie Wilson played it like a lifelong New Englander, nailing Rich Gedman at second base). Carter, Ojeda, and Darling had come home victoriously (I am counting the Kid's years in Quebec). The Series was tied. But the biggest hurdles for the Mets were actually ahead.

"It's not Darling on three days rest that worries me," said Schmidt. "It's Gooden on three days rest. If I were Dave Johnson, I'd give the ball to Rick Aguilera or Sid Fernandez and say, 'Son, go out there and make a name for yourself.'"

Johnson, though, had lost his patience with the gopher balls of both, which he considered lapses of concentration. Fernandez wasn't as notorious as Aguilera (and Rick still had to pitch to a guy named Henderson in the tenth inning at Shea), but El Sid had thrown an unnecessary one to Alan Ashby in the fourth game against Houston, and he had been no mystery to the Red Sox in game two. So, Gooden returned from his shelling on short rest. Ironically, Fernandez was to appear twice more during the Series (not in a starting role), and the Red Sox were to find him nothing short of the second coming of Sidd Finch, or the myth of the old Gooden. He was the hidden key to the rest of the season.

That original Gooden, though, was everything Schmidt feared. Here was someone who, for two whole seasons, controlled the universe of baseball from the pitching mound. He went back and forth between raw heat and Lord Charles, allowing little more than a run per nine innings and striking out ten or so along the way; as games went on, he simply got stronger. If a runner should reach to third with no one out, Dwight had the awesome focus of power to throw nine strikes by the next three hitters (as the Dodgers learned many times). He even taught himself to hit and probably could have gone to the minors and returned in two years as an outfielder with power. He was the prototype of the guy who came down from a higher league. The fact that he didn't get to pitch in the playoffs or World Series was one of the main unfulfilled fantasies of 1984 and '85.

But in 1986 Gooden was not the same pitcher, or even the same batter. Despite Met denials that anything had changed, he was erratic and, at times, hit extremely hard. He seemed confused on the mound. He tired late in games and, on a number of occasions, yielded ninth-inning tying homers. In '84, Mets pitching coach Met Stottlemyre remarked that Gooden had the uncanny ability to make adjustments on the spot. Whereas another pitcher might have to wait till the off-season to change his motion in order to hold runners on, Dwight could hear the message in the fourth and come out and do it in the fifth. Even that ability seemed to have deserted him in '86; he became a raw rookie struggling for even the inklings of mastery more often than at any time previously in his career (except maybe for a few innings at Kingsport and Little Falls in 1982).

During his first two years in the Majors, Gooden was a virtual zen master. He hardly spoke, and what he did say was pragmatic, appropriate, and modest. He had no news; he simply fulfilled the requirements of public speech. For all the effect of his words, he might as well have taken a vow of silence; he was a "silent" teacher. The book about him (*Rookie*) was really a book about someone else, but he didn't mind. People expected it.

Who needed Sidd Finch or Bill Lee's yogic relief pitcher making the baseball disappear and reappear? Gooden was the eye of the storm.

In 1985 at Candlestick I sat among his family. His father was as impassive as Doc, but the young cousins or brothers must have thought Dwight was supposed to be Michael Jackson. They wanted a strikeout on every batter, and when anybody put the ball in play, that was an outrage, a "shuck". A hit was a mistake—"You can't do that; no one can hit Doc!"

Call out the bodyguards. Protect the rock video.

At one point, a friend, or relative, came down with a few baseballs that needed autographing. The family member sitting beside me acted as though he were expected to haul them out to the mound on the spot. "Didn't I tell you never to bother the

Doc when he's at work. Can't you see, man. Doc's operatin'. He's conductin' business; he can't sign no baseballs."

Doc emerged from an underbelly of American black culture, and he transformed its chaos in himself into a functional veneer of calm. As a ballplayer, he was dignified, gallant, and spare. These Goodens didn't even know their kin was playing baseball; they wanted cartoon-like domination, triumph of the nouveau-riche; Dwight even did a rap record of their voice in him.

The explanations for what happened to Gooden in '86 ranged from the banal to the supernatural: the hitters adjusted to him, he didn't have control of the curve any more, he ruined his motion trying to cut down on his leg kick, drugs and other personal-life distractions drained him, he lost motivation with the Mets not needing him to win every time, he had a physical injury (the mysterious ankle?), an undiagnosed disease, or it was simply (Bob Gibson) that no one's that good.

Perhaps no single thing caused the change. After all, Gooden's mastery was not some iron domination of strength; it was a subtle combination of speed, rhythm, and control. Other pitchers threw harder; other pitchers had as good a curve ball. Dwight put it all together in a dance.

Even before word of Gooden's cocaine use came out, some people knew. Apparently the kids in the playgrounds of Tampa got the word, but those playgrounds are a long way from corporate headquarters, and there are very few commuters between them to carry the word. A local friend whose job involves working with athletes who have cocaine problems told me he was certain that was Gooden's problem after watching the Giants bomb him one afternoon at Candlestick. He saw a slight distraction of timing and rhythm, a laboring that wasn't there before, a familiar mild bewilderment in Doc's eyes—because he had never fallen so out of synch before. "What chance did he have, really?" my friend asked me. "He was young, black, wealthy, uneducated, suddenly famous, and he lived in Tampa." But Dwight protested such accusations all season, and even had a drug-testing clause put into his contract.

It makes you wonder if the disease is the drug—or the denial. It also casts a different light on Vida Blue: maybe he never had a chance either. If the great Bob Gibson closed out an era, then Vida unknowingly opened another.

But it will be many a season before we close this one out, for American baseball is merely a fifteen-minute-old puppet show up against the millennial games now being played in Iran, Afghanistan, and Columbia. And most ballplayers are simply grown children, educated by a pop culture for which they are heroes. They are given mentally draining jobs with lots of hollow, meaningless time, and plenty of money. Surely they are set up to be the victims of every big-time global scam; after all, how are they going to outwit poor South American and Southeast Asian farmers or urban drug lords in the battle for the planet's resources; they are mainly worried about "Cardinals" and "Cubs" and how to spend the cash. By the time cocaine reaches suburban Tampa, it is already dressed like the next-door neighbor, and it speaks in whatever street language it needs to get in. Ballplayers might read the papers, but they're the first ones to distrust the information there. They read right through the warnings.

In any case, drugs are not their own answer, nor are they a psychological monolith, transcending all the idiosyncratic events of personal history and culture. Whatever the proximate cause of his struggle (cocaine or some other malaise), an aspect of his unresolved past must have engulfed Doc. He couldn't transform chaos into mastery indefinitely. Every act casts a shadow, and Dwight's first two seasons required some compensation, psychological and physical. That he did as well as he did under the circumstances merely contributes to his myth as a superplayer. The first two seasons he coasted on raw talent and the blessings of both Athena and Zeus; in 1986 the gods opposed him and look what he accomplished! Destiny prescribed that he would lose not only the All-Star Game but two World Series games; sheer guts and ability won seventeen games during the regular season and dueled both Mike Scott and Nolan Ryan by the hair's breadth of a run in the playoffs. If Doc hadn't summoned every ounce of remaining energy and skill he had to force Ryan into extra innings in the fifth game of the playoffs, the Mets never would have made it to the World Series.

I don't believe it for a moment when the Red Sox said after the fifth game, "No one beats us with two pitches." The Dwight Gooden of 1984 and '85 beats them with *either* the curve or the fast ball. The Dwight Gooden of 1986 was on a mission to the Underworld; he was thrashing through the chaos he magically suppressed for two seasons (the same chaos Oil Can struggles with, less successfully). Dwight was a wounded pitcher in the World Series, although we could not see the wounds or know the degrees to which they were physical, psychological, and spiritual. He was pitching with the gods against him, and hits rattled all over Fenway. He was on the most perilous leg of a pilgrimage, far more serious than the game; I mean, two months later he could have been shot dead or had his right arm broken on the streets of Tampa. We don't put much stock in celestial inter-ference these days, but archetypally that was still the work Zeus, in partnership with a malefic Saturn. No wonder he couldn't pitch. That he even survived is a statement of his charisma. ("The sudden fame and fortune he achieved is nice," Frank Cashen would say six months later. "But we sort of robbed him of his youth.")

So, the Mets had to overcome not only their exhaustion and lethargy, and the Sox' two-game lead, they had to play through the deflation of Gooden's invulnerability, a myth so central to the new Mets that it had become almost their team identity. They had to win the big one without him.

To what degree was the World Series uphill for the Mets? Although they did not trail in runs within individual games quite as often as they did during the playoffs, they were behind the Red Sox in the Series itself entering 50 of the 64 innings (all except the first seven innings of the first game, the first two innings of the fifth game, and the first two and last three innings of the seventh game). They actually led in the whole Series for only its final three innings. Several times in the bottom of the tenth of the sixth game they came within one strike of losing it all.

Mike Cieslinski, the inventor of a statistical board game called Pursue the Pennant, tried to recreate the Met comeback in the tenth inning of the sixth game. Using cards representing actual players and dice to randomize outcomes, he sent Carter up to bat against Schiraldi with two outs and no one on. He played all night, but the Red Sox won the Series every time. In his own words, "With two outs—even if you get one or two baserunners—you usually get an out. That's what kept happening: I kept get-ting an out. Actually, I had thoughts of this never happening." But he went back at it the next morning: he rolled the dice 100 times, 200 times, until finally, on his 279th try, the Mets rallied and won. That puts the odds against a Met comeback informally at 278 to 1. Which means, you watch the game from that point 279 times (more than a season and a half), and the Red Sox win 278 times. Why did we get the 279th game on our only try?

Even the one Met who truly walked on water in '69, Ron Swoboda, was astonished. Asked to compared World Series teams, he did some philosophizing and reminiscing: "The champagne dried a little bit and the years went by, but I really enjoyed watching these guys do it because they put their own signature on this one. I can't believe it. They almost killed me. . . . When it was two outs in the bottom of the tenth, my heart was down there in my shoes. I'm trying to figure out some kind of fallback position. I'm thinking, 'Geez, if they don't win it, well at least we're the only ones who did'—all kinds of rationalizations—and all of a sudden you get three base hits, a wild pitch, an error, and I'm screaming, you know, I'm screaming."

When the Mets had two outs and no one on, I stood up and approached the TV, ready to turn it off because I didn't want to watch the Red Sox celebrating. Apparently Keith Hernandez felt the same way because he went back to the manager's office where he watched the most miraculous World Series comeback of all time. In normal circumstances no one comes back from there; in the sixth game of the World Series, definitely not. But all along, Robin was telling me, no, not to worry, that they couldn't lose. Hit after hit proved his faith. He kept saying, "Rich, sit down. Don't even think of it." So much positive energy in such a hopeless cause. Then, as Kevin Mitchell scored the tying run, I yelled myself hoarse; I had watched baseball all my life trying unsuccessfully to root a wild pitch with the tying run on third. Why now, when it mattered most?

This was clearly the same Twilight Zone into which Rick Camp had hit his home run. Mookie Wilson was so faint afterwards he could barely talk. And now that a new season is beginning, baseball has barely yet absorbed it. This was hardball too, but it seemed more like a UFO descended on New York City. And the fans just stayed and cheered the visitation. On an evening begun by Paul Simon singing the National Anthem, and punctuated by a comet-colored second-inning sky-plunger, the inevitable ending had been written.

Too often, in the months afterwards, Mookie has been cheated out of the wonder of that at-bat. In a batting slump, with the whole season on the line and no strikes to give, he fouled off two biting Bob Stanley sinkers, dodged the game-tying wild pitch, and made contact with another sinker, sending it toward first. All that work, plus his intimidating speed, led to Buckner's error. "Mookie the whiff," said a Red Sox fan in typical contempt for both the batter and the pitcher, in an attempt to minimize what happened and make it tolerable. But Wilson well described the drama and intensity inside himself: "When I was up there, I felt like everything was happening in slow motion. I didn't hear the crowd. That was the most I concentrated in one at-bat in my whole career. That at-bat was my career. When it was over, I was drained. That's what I've played all these years for. You dream about that situation, being up with the game on the line. Everything went down to one at-bat. It was the difference between winning and losing. It was perfect."

The parallels between seventh games of two World Series eleven years apart run so spookily close that they suggest the synchronicities of the Lincoln and Kennedy assassinations. Both games followed historic extra-inning contests of sudden reversals of fortune. In both seventh games the Red Sox had a 3–0 lead entering the sixth inning, with a rare left-handed pitcher seemingly in command (in '75 Bill Lee threw the Moon Curve to Tony Perez and suddenly it was 3–2). In 1975 the losing pitcher was Jim Burton, who finished his career on the Mets' Tidewater farm club; in 1986 the losing pitcher was Calvin Schiraldi who spent much of the previous season on Tidewater. (In fact, it seemed a particularly bad omen for the Sox that in a tight seventh game of a World Series they should twice go to the bullpen in late innings and come up with two of their opponent's least effective hurlers in a 26–7 loss to the Phillies the season before, not only Schiraldi but Joe Sambito.)

I would like to think that, over the history of baseball, the Mets and Red Sox are more allies than adversaries—and that their preseason trade of pitchers and fortuitous late-season exhibition game at Fenway united the fortunes of the clubs. Hopefully, the Series will not leave bad blood, but the taunting of Darryl Strawberry by white fans during the fifth game in Boston and the anti-black rioting that swept rural Massachusetts after the seventh game were ominous signs. It would seem, in the wake of Marty Barret and Mookie Wilson visiting the college campuses together to heal those wounds that Al Nipper, still brooding over the fact that Strawberry took his time going around the bases on his culminative seventh-game home run, could have been a little smarter than to threaten and then go out and drill Strawberry with his first spring training pitch to him. Should Rick Aguilera now go after Dave Henderson for showboating on *his* home run?

After midnight in the Met locker room, Sal, the weary local announcer, stands in front of the large white World Series 1986 banner, a hand to his earplug, a towel around his neck, mike held limply, still trying to send up newsfeeds. He goes through Carter and Mazzilli, Hernandez and Knight: ("Fuck the highlights!" Keith says, hugging his blood brother; "you've got the star right here!"). Sal frantically waves for another player to join him, but it is too far into the partying. Then Tim Teufel comes by, still in uniform, carrying the requisite champagne bottle in his fist.

"How do you feel, Tim?" Sal asks, throwing an awkward arm around him. Teufel shakes his head, smiling impishly, then crosses over the camera, and summons another player. It's Kevin Mitchell, the Mets' gravity third-baseman; he's wearing a baseball visor, a gold tee shirt cut off at the shoulders, and orange wrist bands. Teufel slides his right arm around Mitchell's neck, and, gesturing with his fingers on Mitchell's shoulder, says quietly, "Sal, they wrote us off, and we proved them wrong. That's the bottom line." He silently affirms his own sentiment, and then stands there, trying to look diffidently professional, crooking a finger around his bottle, signalling to passing teammates, waiting for the interview to begin. Something catches his eye: "How about the NBC cap?" A technician hands it to him and he adjusts its strap for his head size; meanwhile, Bob Ojeda, wearing a white Mets cap and a warmup jacket, slips in behind him. Smiling sheepishly, he puts his arm around Teufel, and signals Number One with his finger. They all stand there nervously as though waiting to pose for the family album.

"Okay, we're in the weather and then it comes to us," Sal finally says. Teufel throws back his head, takes a drink, and stares bemusedly at the bottle. Then he flips it semi-consciously to the side and lets Mitchell drink.

Sal becomes aware of Ojeda who has circled in front of them, and he shouts, "Bobby O!"

Teufel adds, "The Eatery!" pulls the NBC cap down over his eyes, and repeats the phrase to himself. Ojeda is trying to find his way back into the group from behind, but the banner is in the way, and Teufel and Mitchell are searching for him behind it, lifting the material and tossing it around. This state of chaos worries Sal: "Hey, get out of this! Come over here!" he says.

Ojeda suddenly returns under the banner and asks, "Is this live?"

"Yeah, we're coming through this live," Sal says. Now Mitchell leans in front of Teufel, squeals, and squirts beverage right in Ojeda's face. Ojeda stumbles over forward and struggles to wipe his eyes.

"Here's a towel," Teufel says. "I hate that shit, man," turning to Mitchell in sham outrage. But Mitchell is spraying again, and this time he soaks both Teufel and Sal. Teufel wipes his own face on the announcer's towel, yanks the bottle away from Mitchell, and says, "You're damn getting crazy. This stuff gets in his eyes he can't do the interview." Mitchell is devilishly unimpressed; he simply wants to reload.

"You guys should sing 'New York, New York,'" Sal says, as though to suggest something also crazy but a little less raucous.

Mitchell now has taken on the persona of a show wrestler; he shoots out a forearm, swatting Ojeda squarely on the top of the head. "Put on his gargles!" he barks. "Let him put on his gargles." We see that Ojeda is wearing plastic goggles on a band around his neck. Mitchell has gotten ahold of them and is trying to pull them up onto his eyes. Ojeda is not so much resisting as continuing to press the towel into his eyes, trying to get them opened. "Let me check'em out, man," says Mitchell. And then, to counter any objection, he quickly adds the reason he needs them: "I'm going swimming." He pulls the goggles off, but Ojeda takes them back and sets them in place over his eyes. At this moment, with players wrestling before the camera and Sal pleading, "Wait, wait!" into the microphone, Danny Heep rushes up, puts his hand on the ear plug, and asks deadpan, "You got a problem here?" They all laugh.

Mitchell reaches out for Heep's bottle: "Hey man, let me get one sip." Ojeda, goggles adjusted, stares blankly out into space. Suddenly they are on the air.

"We're back in the Mets' clubhouse: Danny Heep, Bobby Ojeda, Kevin Mitchell—" Sal gesturing to each one as he says the name. The players have not yet noticed this change of focus and are continuing to wrestle with the bottle. " . . . and Tim Teufel, who was classy enough to come on after his big goof in the first game . . . " Mitchell grabs a can of beer from Ojeda's hand, fills his mouth with it, and then explodes it in Heep's face. " . . . but now he's a world champion."

Teufel realizes he's been addressed: "That's right. I'm a world champion, the whole team is, and we're all very excited. Whatever happened in the first game," petulantly, "is all behind us." While he is speaking, Heep has recovered, ducked, and deftly shoved a reloaded Mitchell away. So Mitchell sprays Teufel and Sal.

"O-kay!" says Sal with tired jubilation. He looks around nervously for who's next. "Bobby Ojeda! Here's Bobby Ojeda," he almost shrieks. Ojeda steps forward, so close to the camera he is out of scale, his goggles on, his eyes staring flat out, his right hand raised Hi! as though an outerspaceman saying hello to Earth. Beer cans and bottles are passing back and forth in front of him, and Mitchell squirts him squarely in the eyes as he waves hello to New York. But the goggles are protecting him now. "Hi folks," he says, walking forward into the camera, his hair soaked, foam dripping down his face. Danny Heep pulls down the white banner and tosses it on his head. "I have . . . I have . . . " says Ojeda, pointing to his goggles. Then he presses his face right up against the camera, out of focus, grimacing. When he pulls it off, Sal is gone, the banner is gone, and a very professional acting Teufel has the microphone and is approaching him fresh, as though for the *real* interview: "Bobby, Bobby, how does it feel?"

Ojeda is staggering backward holding up the beer. Then he hears the question: "It feels incredible, Mr. Teufel . . . "

Mitchell steps up, face to face with Ojeda, and spits beer all over him. "It's because he's swimming," he snarls.

"Yes, I *am* swimming. But I don't feel it. I don't feel a thing." Heep is pouring beer on his head from behind. But Ojeda is hot now; he points to his goggles and says, "These are shatterproof, they're . . . " Mitchell unloads in his face again, interrupting him.

"Will you quit drinking my beer, Mr. Mitchell."

Unimpressed, Mitchell fills up and squirts him again. "Do you always act like this, Kevin Mitchell?" asks announcer Teufel.

Protected in goggles, Ojeda points to his own face: "I don't feel a thing. You can buy this at your local supermarket. These are breakproof . . . shatterproof . . . " A new barrage of beer. " . . . spitproof . . . "

"This interview is now over": Teufel.

"Poof . . . poof . . . poof . . . " continues Ojeda, then: "You better cut this."

He staggers away and Mitchell steps forward, turning to reveal the back of his tee shirt on which is sewn in script: "I ONLY HIT ROPES." He shakes the can of beer empty, then points to it and says, "I'm through with you. You're fired!"

So, the 1986 season rushes out through the last ragged end.

Or, as Gary Carter put it later, "In a corner of my mind I will stand forever with my bat cocked, waiting for the two-one pitch from Calvin Schiraldi. It is the bottom of the tenth inning, two out, nobody on base."

With acknowledgement and thanks to the following sources for quoted material: *Mets Inside Pitch* (Ron Swoboda epigraph and Mookie Wilson), *Baseball America* (Mike Cieslinski), George Leonard (from *The Silent Pulse*), *A Dream Season* by Gary Carter and John Hough, Jr. (Gary Carter), and Sportschannel/New York (Mike Schmidt and Ron Swoboda). The locker-room dialogue was transcribed from Satcom I (satellite).

W. P. Kinsella

HOW I GOT MY NICKNAME

For Brian Fawcett, whose story
"My Career with the Leafs" inspired this story.

In the summer of 1951, the summer before I was to
start Grade 12, my polled Hereford calf, Simon Bolivar, won
Reserve Grand Champion at the Des Moines, All-Iowa Cattle
Show and Summer Exposition. My family lived on a hobby-farm
near Iowa City. My father who taught classics at Coe College in
Cedar Rapids, and in spite of that was still the world's number
one baseball fan, said I deserved a reward—I also had a straight
A average in Grade 11 and had published my first short story
that spring. My father phoned his friend Robert Fitzgerald (Fitzgerald, an eminent translator, sometimes phoned my father late
at night and they talked about various ways of interpreting the
tougher parts of *The Iliad*) and two weeks later I found myself
in Fitzgerald's spacious country home outside of New York City,
sharing the lovely old house with the Fitzgeralds, their endless
supply of children, and a young writer from Georgia named Flan-
nery O'Connor. Miss O'Connor was charming, and humorous in
an understated way, and I wish I had talked with her more. About
the third day I was there I admitted to being a published writer
and Miss O'Connor said "You must show me some of your
stories." I never did. I was seventeen, overweight, diabetic, and
bad-complexioned. I alternated between being terminally shy and
obnoxiously brazen. I was nearly always shy around the Fitzgeralds and Miss O'Connor. I was also terribly homesick, which
made me appear more silent and outlandish than I knew I was.
I suspect I am the model for Enoch Emery, the odd, lonely coun-

try boy in Miss O'Connor's novel *Wise Blood*. But that is another story.

On a muggy August morning, the first day of a Giant home stand at the Polo Grounds, I prepared to travel into New York. I politely invited Miss O'Connor to accompany me, but she, even at that early date had to avoid sunlight and often wore her wide-brimmed straw hat, even indoors. I set off much too early and though terrified of the grimy city and shadows that seemed to lurk in every doorway, arrived at the Polo Grounds over two hours before game time. It was raining gently and I was one of about two dozen fans in the ballpark. A few players were lethargically playing catch, a coach was hitting fungos to three players in right field. I kept edging my way down the rows of seats until I was right behind the Giants dugout.

The Giants were thirteen games behind the Dodgers and the pennant race appeared all but over. A weasel-faced bat boy, probably some executive's nephew, I thought, noticed me staring wide-eyed at the players and the playing field. He curled his lip at me, then stuck out his tongue. He mouthed the words "Take a picture, it'll last longer," adding something at the end that I could only assume to be uncomplimentary.

Fired by the insult I suddenly mustered all my bravado and called out "Hey, Mr Durocher?" Leo Durocher, the Giants manager, had been standing in the third base coach's box not looking at anything in particular. I was really impressed. That's the grand thing about baseball, I thought. Even a manager in a pennant race can take time to daydream. He didn't hear me. But the bat boy did, and stuck out his tongue again.

I was overpowered by my surroundings. Though I'd seen a lot of major league baseball I'd never been in the Polo Grounds before. The history of the place . . . "Hey, Mr Durocher," I shouted.

Leo looked up at me with a baleful eye. He needed a shave, and the lines around the corners of his mouth looked like ruts.

"What is it, Kid?"

"Could I hit a few?" I asked hopefully, as if I was begging to stay up an extra half hour. "You know, take a little batting practice?"

"Sure, Kid. Why not?" and Leo smiled with one corner of his mouth. "We want all our fans to feel like part of the team."

From the box seat where I'd been standing, I climbed up on

the roof of the dugout and Leo helped me down onto the field.

Leo looked down into the dugout. The rain was stopping. On the other side of the park a few of the Phillies were wandering onto the field. "Hey, George," said Leo, staring into the dugout, "throw the kid here a few pitches. Where are you from, son?"

It took me a few minutes to answer because I experienced this strange, lightheaded feeling, as if I had too much sun. "Near to Iowa City, Iowa," I managed to say in a small voice. Then "You're going to win the pennant, Mr. Durocher. I just know you are."

"Well, thanks, Kid," said Leo modestly, "we'll give it our best shot."

George was George Bamberger, a stocky rookie who had seen limited action. "Bring the kid a bat, Andy," Leo said to the bat boy. The bat boy curled his lip at me but slumped into the dugout, as Bamberger and Sal Yvars tossed the ball back and forth.

The bat boy brought me a black bat. I was totally unprepared for how heavy it was. I lugged it to the plate and stepped into the right hand batter's box. Bamberger delivered an easy, looping, batting-practice pitch. I drilled it back up the middle.

"Pretty good, Kid," I heard Durocher say.

Bamberger threw another easy one and I fouled it off. The third pitch was a little harder. I hammered it to left.

"Curve him," said Durocher.

He curved me. Even through my thick glasses the ball looked as big as a grapefruit, illuminated like a small moon. I whacked it and it hit the right field wall on one bounce.

"You weren't supposed to hit that one," said Sal Yvars.

"You're pretty good, Kid," shouted Durocher from the third base box. "Give him your best stuff, George."

Over the next fifteen minutes I batted about .400 against George Bamberger, and Roger Bowman, including a home run into the left centrefield stands. The players on the Giants bench were watching me with mild interest often looking up from the books most of them were reading.

"I'm gonna put the infield out now," said Durocher. "I want you to run out some of your hits."

Boy, here I was batting against the real New York Giants. I wished I'd worn a new shirt instead of the horizontally striped red and white one I had on, which made me look heftier than I really was. Bowman threw a sidearm curve and I almost broke my back swinging at it. But he made the mistake of coming right back with the same pitch. I looped it behind third where it landed soft as a sponge, and trickled off toward the stands—I'd seen the play hundreds of times—a stand-up double. But when I was still twenty feet from second base Eddie Stanky was waiting with the ball. "Slide!" somebody yelled, but I just skidded to a stop, stepping out of the baseline to avoid the tag. Stanky whapped me anyway, a glove to the ribs that would have made Rocky Marciano or Ezzard Charles proud.

When I got my wind back Durocher was standing, hands on hips, staring down at me.

"Why the hell didn't you slide, Kid?"

"I can't," I said, a little indignantly. "I'm diabetic, I have to avoid stuff like that. If I cut myself, or even bruise badly, it takes forever to heal."

"Oh," said Durocher. "Well, I guess that's okay then."

"You shouldn't tag people so hard," I said to Stanky. "Somebody could get hurt."

"Sorry, Kid," said Stanky. I don't think he apologized very often. I noticed that his spikes were filed. But I found later that he knew a lot about F. Scott Fitzgerald. His favourite story was "Babylon Revisited" so that gave us a lot in common; I was a real Fitzgerald fan; Stanky and I became friends even though both he and Durocher argued against reading *The Great Gatsby* as an allegory.

"Where'd you learn your baseball?" an overweight coach who smelled strongly of snuff, and bourbon, said to me.

"I live near Iowa City, Iowa," I said in reply.

Everyone wore question marks on their faces. I saw I'd have to elaborate. "Iowa City is within driving distance of Chicago, St. Louis, Milwaukee, and there's minor league ball in Cedar Rapids, Omaha, Kansas City. Why there's barely a weekend my dad and I don't go somewhere to watch professional baseball."

"Watch?" said Durocher.

"Well, we talk about it some too. My father is a real student of the game. Of course we only talk in Latin when we're on the road, it's a family custom."

"Latin?" said Durocher.

"Say something in Latin," said Whitey Lockman, who had

wandered over from first base.

"The Etruscans have invaded all of Gaul," I said in Latin.

"Their fortress is on the banks of the river," said Bill Rigney, who had been filling in at third base.

"Velle est posse," I said.

"Where there's a will there's a way," translated Durocher.

"Drink Agri Cola . . . " I began.

"The farmer's drink," said Sal Yvars, slapping me on the back, but gently enough not to bruise me. I guess I looked a little surprised.

"Most of us are more than ballplayers," said Alvin Dark, who had joined us. "In fact the average player on this squad is fluent in three languages."

"Watch?" said Durocher, getting us back to baseball. "You *watch* a lot of baseball, but where do you play?"

"I've never played in my life," I replied. "But I have a photographic memory. I just watch how different players hold their bat, how they stand. I try to emulate Enos Slaughter and Joe DiMaggio.

"Can you field?" said Durocher.

"No."

"No?"

"I've always just watched the hitters. I've never paid much attention to the fielders."

He stared at me as if I had spoken to him in an unfamiliar foreign language.

"Everybody fields," he said. "What position do you play?"

"I've never played," I reiterated. "My health is not very good."

"Cripes," he said, addressing the sky. "You drop a second Ted Williams on me and he tells me he can't field." Then to Alvin Dark: "Hey, Darky, throw a few with the kid here. Get him warmed up."

In the dugout Durocher pulled a thin, black glove from an equipment bag and tossed it to me. I dropped it. The glove had no discernable padding in it. The balls Dark threw hit directly on my hand, when I caught them, which was about one out of three. "Ouch!" I cried. "Don't throw so hard."

"Sorry, Kid," said Alvin Dark and threw the next one a little easier. If I really heaved I could just get the ball back to him. I have always thrown like a non-athletic girl. I could feel my hand bloating inside the thin glove. After about ten pitches, I pulled my hand out. It looked as though it had been scalded.

"Don't go away, Kid," said Leo. "In fact why don't you sit in the dugout with me. What's your name anyway?"

"W. P. Kinsella," I said.

"Your friends call you W?"

"My father calls me William, and my mother . . . " but I let my voice trail off. I didn't think Leo Durocher would want to know my mother still called me Bunny.

"Jeez," said Durocher. "You need a nickname, Kid. Bad."

"I'll work on it," I said.

I sat right beside Leo Durocher all that stifling afternoon in the Polo Grounds as the Giants swept a doubleheader from the Phils, the start of a sixteen-game streak that was to lead to the October 3, 1951 Miracle of Coogan's Bluff. I noticed right away that the Giants were all avid readers. In fact, the *New York Times* Best Seller Lists, and the *Time* and *Newsweek* lists of readable books and an occasional review were taped to the walls of the dugout. When the Giants were in the field I peeked at the covers of the books the players sometimes read between innings. Willie Mays was reading *The Cruel Sea* by Nicholas Monsarrat. Between innings Sal Maglie was deeply involved in Carson McCuller's new novel *The Ballad of the Sad Cafe.* "I sure wish we could get that Cousin Lyman to be our mascot," he said to me when he saw me eyeing the bookjacket, referring to the hunchbacked dwarf who was the main character in the novel. "We need something to inspire us," he added. Alvin Dark slammed down his copy of *Requiem for a Nun* and headed for the on-deck circle.

When the second game ended, a sweaty and sagging Leo Durocher took me by the arm. "There's somebody I want you to meet, Kid," he said. Horace Stoneham's office was furnished in wine-coloured leather sofas and overstuffed horsehair chairs. Stoneham sat behind an oak desk as big as the dugout, enveloped in cigar smoke.

"I've got a young fellow here I think we should sign for the stretch drive," Durocher said. "He can't field or run, but he's as pure a hitter as I've ever seen. He'll make a hell of a pinch hitter."

"I suppose you'll want a bonus?" growled Stoneham.

"I do have something in mind," I said. Even Durocher was

not nearly as jovial as he had been. Both men stared coldly at me. Durocher leaned over and whispered something to Stoneham.

"How about $6,000," Stoneham said.

"What I'd really like . . . " I began.

"Alright, $10,000, but not a penny more."

"Actually, I'd like to meet Bernard Malamud. I thought you could maybe invite him down to the park. Maybe get him to sign a book for me?" They both looked tremendously relieved.

"Bernie and me and this kid Salinger are having supper this evening," said Durocher. "Why don't you join us?"

"You mean J. D. Salinger?" I said.

"Jerry's a big Giant fan," he said. "The team Literary Society read *Catcher in the Rye* last month. We had a panel discussion on it for eight hours on the train to St. Louis."

Before I signed the contract I phoned my father.

"No reason you can't postpone your studies until the end of the season," he said. "It'll be good experience for you. You'll gather a lot of material you can write about later. Besides, baseball players are the real readers of America."

I got my first hit off Warren Spahn, a solid single up the middle. Durocher immediately replaced me with a pinch runner. I touched Ralph Branca for a double, the ball went over Duke Snider's head, hit the wall and bounced half way back to the infield. Anyone else would have had an inside the park homer. I wheezed into second and was replaced. I got into 38 of the final 42 games. I hit 11 for 33, and was walked four times. And hit once. That was the second time I faced Warren Spahn. He threw a swishing curve that would have gone behind me if I hadn't backed into it. I slouched off toward first holding my ribs.

"You shouldn't throw at batters like that," I shouted, "someone could get seriously hurt. I'm diabetic, you know." I'd heard that Spahn was into medical texts and interested in both human and veterinary medicine.

"Sorry," he shouted back. "If I'd known I wouldn't have thrown at you. I've got some good linament in the clubhouse. Come see me after the game. By the way I hear you're trying to say that *The Great Gatsby* is an allegory.

"The way I see it, it is," I said. "You see the eyes of the optometrist on the billboard are really the eyes of God looking down on a fallen world . . . "

"Alright, alright," said the umpire, Beans Reardon, "let's get on with the game. By the way, Kid, I don't think it's an allegory either. A statement on the human condition, perhaps. But not an allegory."

The players wanted to give me some nickname other than "Kid." Someone suggested "Ducky" in honour of my running style. "Fats" said somebody else. I made a note to remove his bookmark between innings. Several other suggestions were downright obscene. Baseball players, in spite of their obsession with literature and the arts, often have a bawdy sense of humour.

"How about 'Moonlight,'" I suggested. I'd read about an old time player who stopped for a cup of coffee with the Giants half a century before, who had that nickname.

"What the hell for?" said Monty Irvin, who in spite of the nickname preferred to be called Monford or even by his second name Merrill. "You got to have a reason for a nickname. You got to earn it. Still, anything's better than W.P."

"It was only a suggestion," I said. I made a mental note not to tell Monford what I knew about *his* favourite author, Erskine Caldwell.

As it turned out I didn't earn a nickname until the day we won the pennant.

As every baseball fan knows the Giants went into the bottom of the ninth in the deciding game of the pennant playoff trailing the Dodgers 4-1.

"Don't worry," I said to Durocher, "everything's going to work out." If he heard me he didn't let on.

But was everything going to work out? And what part was I going to play in it? Even though I'd contributed to the Giants' amazing stretch drive, I didn't belong. Why am I here? I kept asking myself. I had some vague premonition that I was about to change history. I meant I wasn't a ballplayer. I was a writer. Here I was about to go into Grade 12 and I was already planning to do my master's thesis on F. Scott Fitzgerald.

I didn't have time to worry further as Alvin Dark singled. Don Mueller, in his excitement had carried his copy of *The Mill on the Floss* out to the on-deck circle. He set the resin bag on top of it, stalked to the plate and singled, moving Dark to second.

I was flabbergasted when Durocher called Monford Irvin back and said to me "Get in there, Kid."

It was at that moment that I knew why I was there. I would indeed change history. One stroke of the bat and the score would be tied. I eyed the left field stands as I nervously swung two bats to warm up. I was nervous but not scared. I never doubted my prowess for one moment. Years later Johnny Bench summed it up for both athletes and writers when he talked about a successful person having to have an *inner conceit.* It never occurred to me until days later that I might have hit into a double or triple play, thus ending it and *really* changing history.

When I did take my place in the batter's box, I pounded the plate and glared out at Don Newcombe. I wished that I shaved so I could give him a stubble-faced stare of contempt. He curved me and I let it go by for a ball. I fouled the next pitch high into the first base stands. A fastball was low. I fouled the next one outside third. I knew he didn't want to go to a full count: I crowded the plate a little looking for the fastball. He curved me. Nervy. But the curveball hung, sat out over the plate like a cantaloupe. I waited an extra millisecond before lambasting it. In that instant the ball broke in on my hands; it hit the bat right next to my right hand. It has been over thirty years but I still wake deep in the night, my hands vibrating, burning from Newcombe's pitch. The bat shattered into kindling. The ball flew in a polite loop as if it had been tossed by a five-year-old; it landed soft as a creampuff in Peewee Reese's glove. One out.

I slumped back to the bench.

"Tough luck, Kid," said Durocher, patting my shoulder. "There'll be other chances to be a hero."

"Thanks, Leo," I said.

Whitey Lockman doubled. Dark scored. Mueller hurt himself sliding into third. Rafael Noble went in to run for Mueller. Charlie Dressen replaced Newcombe with Ralph Branca. Bobby Thomson swung bats in the on-deck circle.

As soon as umpire Jorda called time-in, Durocher leapt to his feet, and before Bobby Thomson could take one step toward the plate, Durocher called him back.

"Don't do that!" I yelled, suddenly knowing why I was *really* there. But Durocher ignored me. He was beckoning with a big-knuckled finger to another reserve player, a big outfielder who was tearing up the American Association when they brought him up late in the year. He was 5 for 8 as a pinch hitter.

Durocher was already up the dugout steps heading toward the umpire to announce the change. The outfielder from the American Association was making his way down the dugout, hopping along over feet and ankles. He'd be at the top of the step by the time Durocher reached the umpire.

As he skipped by me, the last person between Bobby Thomson and immortality, I stuck out my foot. The outfielder from the American Association went down like he'd been poleaxed. He hit his face on the top step of the dugout, crying out loud enough to attract Durocher's attention.

The trainer hustled the damaged player to the clubhouse. Durocher waved Bobby Thomson to the batter's box. And the rest is history. After the victory celebration I announced my retirement blaming it on a damaged wrist. I went back to Iowa and listened to the World Series on the radio.

All I have to show that I ever played in the major leagues is my one-line entry in *The Baseball Encyclopedia:*

W.P. KINSELLA   Kinsella, William Patrick "Tripper" BR TR
5'9" 185 lbs. B. Apr. 14, 1934 Onamata, Ia.

	G	AB	H	2B	3B	HR	HR %	R	RBI	BB	SO	EA	Pinch Hit BA	AB	H
1951 NY N	38	33	11	2	0	2	6.0	0	8	4	4	0	.333	33	11

I got my outright release in the mail the week after the World Series ended. Durocher had scrawled across the bottom: "Good luck, Kid. By the way, *The Great Gatsby* is *not* an allegory."

Nancy Willard

---

from
THINGS INVISIBLE TO SEE

In a small Michigan town on the eve of World War II, a young man and woman share a love that is shadowed by tragedy, yet lighted by powers beyond the real. To preserve their future, the young man makes a wager with Death, pitting a local sandlot team against the greatest players who ever lived.

Than When We First Begun

The crucifix on the wall: a broken sleeper.

Through the half-open window drifted sounds from the street: a car careening around the corner, its radio screaming "I got spurs that jingle jangle jingle."

This room is larger than the one I had when I was here, said Clare.

This room is the ward, said the Ancestress. *What do you see?*

I see two rows of houses with lamps burning in all the windows, answered Clare.

Those are the patients whose wounds are healing. Tomorrow they will gather around the radio to hear the game they wanted to play. Your game. Is that all you see, daughter?

They were entering a private room. Clare did not need to ask whose it was.

I see a dark house. Is Ben dying?

Everything alive looks dead and everything dead looks alive, said the Ancestress. *Daughter, his spirit is hiding.*

They floated toward Ben.

What does he love best in the world? asked the Ancestress.
Baseball, said Clare. *Summer.*
You've forgotten what he loves most.
What?
You. Go into his house, daughter; and breathe on all his lamps. But do not linger. The darkness of a house that is being abandoned is like no other darkness on earth.

Clare let herself in.

She never imagined that Ben's life would look like this: a dark corridor, off which opened dank rooms behind doors rotting on their hinges. The sconces in every room were black with soot. But the gas was still on. The lamps would light for her, if the gas didn't kill her first.

She breathed on the first lamp and it glowed softly. The tiniest pilot light awoke at the bottom. She hurried on to the second, and it too awoke at her breath and encouraged the third, which flamed quicker and brighter than the others. She began to feel ill, as if she were trapped in a mine. The air was poisonous. She breathed the fourth lamp to life and the fifth and heard the Ancestress calling her.

Come back now, daughter, or you will never come back.

Once outside, she turned to look at him. Every room was sending out a warm, clear light.

When Hal arrived at the airstrip early in the morning, his heart sank a little. He would have preferred a train, with its ponderous courtesies, not this six-seater, this toy. The pilot, a young man with sandy hair and a sleepy expression, took his valise.

"You're traveling light," he remarked.

"Presents for my family," said Hal. "I can't stay long."

"Oh, that's nice. I got some jewelry in Santa Fe for my mother."

Hal thought of the stuffed horned toad mounted on a piece of petrified wood he was bringing for Davy. The little box of minerals for Clare and Helen. Clare would love the names: desert rose, Apache tears.

"We'll stow this in back," said the pilot. "There's not much room under the seats."

"But I'm the only passenger," said Hal.

The pilot nodded. "It's you and me and my copilot and the

cargo."

Hal wondered where they were taking the cargo—it was packed in three steel boxes, padlocked and unmarked. To Willow Run? He wanted to ask how many stops they'd be making between here and Willow Run, but these last months had taught him to mind his own business.

He climbed in behind the copilot, a thin, blond man with protruding teeth who reminded Hal of a white rabbit.

"Nice day for flying," the rabbit said to Hal. "You'll get a nice view of the sun rising over the Sangre de Cristo mountains. I saw a mountain goat once. You hardly ever see them so well on the ground."

The plane taxied for takeoff, and Hal peered out of the window, not wanting to miss the goat if it was there. He would tell Clare and Helen about the goat and about the aspens shaking their leaves like coins and about these two men and their mysterious cargo. He would walk into the house around supper time, just walk in. No calling beforehand, no letter announcing his arrival. Just walk in, calling, "Hi. I'm home."

Father Legg ran up to Clare.

"You're the second miracle," he said and hugged her.

The first miracle, he told her, was Ben. He was wide awake. Too weak to play, the doctor said, but wide awake. And though it was still too early to say for sure, he appeared to have lost neither speech nor memory nor movement.

"What did he talk about?" asked Clare.

"The game. He can't think of anything else."

"Of course," said Clare.

"The other team hasn't arrived yet," said Father Legg. He avoided uttering the name Dead Knights. "We're warming up. I hope the crowd doesn't make you nervous."

No, she wasn't nervous. No. Because there was only the game and the no-game, the players and the watchers, the inside and the outside. Right now only the inside mattered. The people in the bleachers rustled like so many blades of grass, faceless, innumerable.

The very hairs of your head are numbered, said God.

"Here are your positions," said Father Legg, addressing the little group on the bench. He could not accustom himself to seeing the women in slacks and shirts. Look like they all work in a defense plant, he thought. "And we would especially like to welcome Sol Lieberman and Mr. Clackett."

The two grinned, their right arms in nearly identical casts.

"Sol will coach first base and Mr. Clackett will coach third. Please—give me your attention. Mrs. Teresa Bacco, first base. Mrs. Schoonmaker, second base. Mrs. Lieberman, third. Mrs. Henrietta Bacco, shortstop. Ernestina, you're our catcher."

He wanted a tight outfield, he told them. He was counting on Mrs. LaMont in center and Mrs. Clackett in left. Willie would play right field. Wanda and Helen would wait on the bench in case they were needed.

"And Clare Bishop will pitch," he added with a grin. A current of warm feeling ran through the women. "And you all know the good news about Ben."

He lowered his voice.

"Dear Lord, Who knowest our needs before we ask them, be with us all, now and in the world to come. Ladies—and Willie—take your positions."

Kitty helped Ernestina into her chest protector, and Ernestina laughed nervously and said she felt like an old crawdaddy rigged up like that, and then they all fanned out and trotted to their places. Helen and Wanda made themselves comfortable on the bench.

Poor Wanda, thought Father Legg. She feels useless.

"Wanda, let's see you take a few cuts at the ball," he said gently.

Wanda took her stance, knees flexed, at home plate. Clare did not move. The two women stared at each other.

"What's wrong?" asked Father Legg.

"I was just thinking, this is a funny place for us to meet," said Clare.

"Good heavens!" exclaimed Father Legg. "I thought you knew each other."

Out in left field, Willie shaded his eyes. Were they talking about him? Or was Father Legg giving his pitch on love?

Suddenly the murmurs of the crowd ceased. Wanda let the bat drop. The air grew faintly chill, as if rain were not far off—yet not rain, either, but the dank moisture on the undersides of stones.

"They're here," said Father Legg.

They did not run onto the field. They simply appeared, as if they had broken through a wall of air, or an invisible ray into visibility. First, Durkee, tugging on his visored cap, in his old maroon jacket with "AA Pioneers" in white script on the back. Then the players: big, slow-moving men in the uniforms of the teams they had served. They lumbered onto the field and their feet touched the earth, yet the earth did not take note of them; they raised no dust, disturbed no blade of grass.

Lord have mercy on us, thought Father Legg. They've got Lou Gehrig on first.

And yet he was not as Father Legg remembered him. This man was a shell, its passenger gone; tossed through hurricanes, through deep silences, it had washed ashore intact, luminous, dead.

Their coach strolled over to Father Legg and offered his hand; Father Legg shook it gingerly.

"My name's Death," he said.

"I know," said Father Legg.

"Both of us in black today," Death observed with a smile.

Father Legg said nothing.

"I see you're expecting an easy three innings. You're giving the women a chance."

"A bus accident," said Father Legg. His mouth felt dry. "Everyone was hurt. Nobody killed, fortunately."

"Fortunately," said Death. "I believe most of my players are familiar to you," he added.

Father Legg nodded.

"I never thought I'd live to see Christy Mathewson pitch again. What did he die of?"

"TB," said Death. "Naturally, it doesn't bother him now."

"Naturally," said Father Legg.

"Those who play for me never tire. They never get hurt."

"Very convenient," said Father Legg.

"So many wanted to come. You can imagine. They haven't picked up a bat and ball since the day they died. Durkee was ecstatic. Not all of you can keep your positions, I told them. And they still begged to come. The pitchers even offered to play in the outfield. Baseball was their whole life."

"Do they need to warm up?"

"Some things you never forget," said Death. "Baseball is one of them."

What were the others? Father Legg wondered. Once he would have said "love." Now it did not seem that simple.

The nurse wheeled the radio toward Ben's bed and stopped in the middle of the room.

"I'm sorry. The plug won't reach. We'll push all the beds down to this end."

By the time she found the station, the announcer was half-way through the lineup.

"Mrs. LaMont, center field."

"Give it to 'em, Kitty!" shouted Mr. LaMont.

"And Willie Harkissian in right field. And now the lineup for the Dead Knights."

A hush fell over the room.

"Starting pitcher is Christy Mathewson of the New York Giants. At first base, Lou Gehrig, New York Yankees. At second base, Joe McGinnity, New York Giants."

"Lord," said Mr. Lieberman. "Not Iron Man McGinnity."

"At third base, Eddie Plank of the Philadelphia A's."

"They're playing the wrong positions," said Ben.

"There's a reason for it," said Mr. LaMont. "There's a reason for everything."

"At shortstop," the announcer went on, "Hughie Jennings of the Baltimore Orioles."

"The ee-yah man," said Mr. Schoonmaker. "I used to think the world of him."

"In center field, Rube Waddell of the Philadelphia A's. In left field, Big Dan Brouthers—"

"Rube Waddell!" exclaimed Mr. Bacco. "He's the guy who used to run off the field to chase fire engines."

"In right field, Ross Youngs of the New York Giants. And the catcher: Moses Fleetwood Walker."

"Who's he?" asked Mr. Bacco.

"He played with the Chicago Lincolns," said Stilts.

"There's a Negro on this team?"

"He's dead, isn't he?" said Stilts. "This ain't the majors."

They were flying over Lake Erie when Hal realized he was listening to the engine of the plane. The steady hum had shifted into a lower pitch. then a quick, polite cough. Another, and another. And then it hummed as before, but Hal kept listening, noting the smallest changes in its voice. The two pilots had stopped talking and were listening, too. As the hum steadied itself, Hal felt his muscles unclench.

Whef-a-whef-a-whef.

The pilot checked the fuel gauge.

Whef-a-whef.

"Engine trouble?" inquired Hal.

"Not really," said the pilot.

They were all listening intently now, and each knew the others were listening too, and waiting for the cough in the motor, the rattle in the chest, blood in the urine, numbness in the leg, a dizzy spell, a lump: Doctor, will I die?

Christy Mathewson, five years dead, translucent as a leaf through which the sun scatters shadows, had not lost his pinpoint control. He hurled a fastball at Mrs. LaMont, who swung under it and missed.

"Makes 'em hit on the ground," observed Mr. Clackett to Sol. "It's a damned hard pitch to hit in the air."

"God help us if he throws his knuckleball," said Father Legg.

Dear Lord, he whispered, Dear Lord Who stopped the sun for Joshua, Thou knowest the score is three to nothing in the bottom of the first. Thou knowest the Dead Knights are winning. Stop the ball, Lord, so that Mrs. LaMont may hit it.

But the Lord did not stop the ball, and Mrs. LaMont struck out.

"It's a bad time to need the bedpan," said Charley. "There must be fifty people in here."

"Do you have to—?" asked the nurse.

"No," he answered quickly.

The nurses from the floor and the ambulatory patients from the private rooms had gathered in the ward. That nurse's aide by the door—Ben was sure he'd met her before, in an earlier life.

"I'm Ginny," she said. "Remember?"

Of course. How could he have forgotten?

"The kid with the St. Anthony medal—remember?" said

Ginny. "He finally went home. He asked if I'd take him for a ride in my old Studebaker next time he's in the hospital."

"He's probably listening to the game right now," said Ben.

"There's one out in the bottom of the first," said the announcer, "and three-zip is the score. This is a big game for the Rovers. 'Course, it's a big game for the Dead Knights, too . . . Mrs. Schoonmaker's at the plate. There's the windup—the pitch— it's an easy grounder toward first base. Gehrig fields it, steps on the bag. That's two out, nobody on."

It was terribly quiet in the ward. Everyone seemed to stop breathing at once.

"Mathewson winds up. The pitch—it's a slider. Mrs. Lieberman swings and misses. Strike one."

Ben climbed off his bed and threaded his way to the door and nudged Ginny.

"Where are your car keys?"

"In my coat pocket. Why?"

"Don't ask. Where are you parked?"

"In the first row behind the hospital, but—"

Clare stood up and walked behind the dugout. If she was going to cry, she wanted to get it over and done with, out of sight. A fly buzzed at her ear; she swatted it fiercely.

Don't, daughter. You know me.

"Dear lady," whispered Clare, "can't you go into the ball and make us hit it? Or make them not hit it?"

I can't give you anything you don't already have, murmured the Ancestress.

"You got into the knife."

Ben has a way with a knife. He just hadn't discovered it.

She could still taste the dust from the field, chalky, all the way down her throat. "I don't have a way with the ball," said Clare.

True, said the Ancestress. *Therefore, do as Ben does. Put some stuff on it. The Dead Knights can never hit a ball with some stuff on it.*

"What kind of stuff?" asked Clare.

The stuff of being alive. Morning, evening, the first snow and the last snow, bells, daisies, hubcaps, silver dollars, ice cream, hummingbirds, love.

Clare drew a deep breath. "How do you put that kind of stuff on a ball?"

You say it very softly over the ball before you throw it.

She heard Father Legg calling her.

And when you pitch to Mr. Gehrig, say "Mother." There's nothing he wouldn't do for his mother.

His clothes—where were his clothes? The nurse's lounge was empty. Ben darted in and opened the closet. Nothing but a blue raincoat and a pink silk scarf. He pulled them on over his hospital gown.

He had almost reached the stairs when Ginny grabbed his arm.

"My raincoat! My scarf! Where are you going in my clothes?"

"I'm going to tie up the ball game."

"You can't go! You haven't been discharged."

"That's why I took your clothes. Ginny, please!"

"You can't go—"

"I can't wait to be discharged. I'm needed *now*," he cried and yanked himself free of her grasp. She let him go, down the stairs and through the lobby past the receptionist and out the front door, past the patients in wheelchairs who were brought out every afternoon for fresh air and a change of scene. He did not stop running till he reached the parking lot. Ginny's car. Ginny's car—which was Ginny's car?

A window opened on the sixth floor, and her voice called out, "It's over there, to your right, the blue one."

Thank you, Ginny. Thank you, car. Thank you, God. Ben drove out of the lot and headed toward the ballpark.

By the time Youngs and Jennings had struck out, everybody in the ward was cheering, and everybody in the bleachers who knew anything about baseball realized one thing:

They'd never seen a ball behave like this one.

"Will you look at Bishop's unorthodox delivery!" exclaimed the announcer. "A high kick, then she bends down as if she's talking to the ball. Good breaking pitch by Bishop. Strike two. Two quick strikes on McGinnity, two out in the top of the second. . . . Watch that pitch. McGinnity is swinging at her motion, not at the ball. Halfway into the swing he decides not to swing.

Ball one. It's one and two."

Over the ball, Clare whispered: "A cold beer. Your first home run."

The ball sped away and McGinnity started to swing, then stepped back as if he'd gotten a whiff of something it was carrying, something that took his eye off the ball, off the game, everything.

Strike three.

Clare glanced up and saw, over the bleachers, a vast, silent throng that receded as if on invisible waves, the women in white, the men in black, the lovely fabric of their presence growing faint among the far-off dead, turning in those farthest from her to feathers, wings, the faces of birds.

Willie was bending over the drinking fountain behind the bleachers when someone tapped him lightly on the shoulder.

"Willie," said Death, "nobody appreciates you."

"I know," said Willie. Immediately he felt embarrassed. He hadn't meant to say it right out.

"You're a good, steady worker. You're smart. What's a girl like Marsha in the eyes of the great world? She'll marry a doctor and live unhappily ever after. There are thousands of girls more beautiful where I come from. Don't look so surprised. I know both the living and the dead; they all come to me eventually."

Willie rolled the water around in his mouth thoughtfully, as if he were judging a fine wine. A cheer from the bleachers startled him.

"Matty just walked Mrs. Henrietta Bacco," remarked Death.

"I'm up now," said Willie.

"I give good benefits, Willie," said Death. "Wonderful vacations. Willie, I want *you*. Join my club and see the world. I've got a job for you."

"What kind of job?"

"I want you to keep my records, plead my cause. Snuff out hope wherever you find it. It's what you've always done, Willie. And you can start right this minute."

"No, thanks," said Willie.

"Willie, last night Mr. Jackson was arrested. He named you."

"He named me?"

"There will be a trial, of course. These are patriotic times.

You won't get off easily."

The pilot broke the silence.

"The fuel gauge has been reading empty for the last hour," he observed. "According to my instruments, we should all be dead."

None of them was ever to know for certain exactly what happened next. The pilot said it was the clouds; they played tricks on you. Made you think you were seeing whole cities, armies. The co-pilot blamed it on magnetic currents: there were currents you could hit up there that made all your instruments malfunction.

Only Hal believed his eyes. The engines were silent. But under the wing he saw the ghostly shapes of children, animals, birds, bearing them up.

Willie struck out, and the crowd roared its grief: *"Awwwwwww."*

"You see, Willie," murmured Death as Willie walked toward the dugout. "You have a calling."

"What's the pay?" asked Willie.

"Every living thing in the world shall be yours."

"Then I'm your man," said Willie. "But I'm not packed."

"No need to pack," said Death. "Everything you'll ever need is furnished."

From his pocket he drew a coin—a skull on one side, a man in a winged cap on the other—and slipped it into Willie's hand.

"Come."

"The game's not over," said Willie. "And you're winning."

"We're losing," said Death. "Can't you see? Do you think Gehrig and Waddell and McGinnity and Jennings couldn't hit if they wanted to? Do you think Matty had to walk Mrs. Bacco? They want the living to win. Even the umpire wants the living to win. They remember how it was. All the pain, all the trouble —they'd choose it again—they'd go extra innings into infinity for the chance to be alive again."

It seemed to Helen that she heard Hal singing, heard him so clearly behind the murmur of the crowd that she could even make out the words:

*"When we've been there ten thousand years
Bright Shining as the sun—"*

She looked around for Grandpa, knowing full well he was in the bleachers. It was Hal's voice, she was sure of it now, and her heart fluttered a little. She had not heard any sound that far off since the last snowfall. All spring she'd heard the usual sounds, the chirp of crickets but not the silence of crickets; the drumming of rain on the roof but not the plotting of rain in the clouds. And now she heard Hal's voice drawing nearer and nearer like an approaching parade.

"What does it mean?" she wondered, and Father Legg next to her said, "It's a miracle," as Clare swung and connected.

The next moment Helen was shouting at him. "Who is that coming out on the field?"

It was a figure to make the dead sit up and take notice: a tall woman in a blue raincoat, a pink babushka and slippers, and as she ran she threw off her clothes, one garment at a time. First the raincoat; the hospital gown she wore underneath did not even reach to her knees. When the babushka was tossed away, the players gaped in astonishment, and Clare, digging her toe into first base, gave a shout.

"It's Ben!"

In the ward, the announcer's voice crackled with excitement.

"Folks, that's two on for the Rovers, only one away. A home run now would tie it up, and ladies and gentlemen, coming to bat"—his voice broke—"is Ben Harkissian!"

"Who?" exclaimed Charley.

"Listen!" hissed Ginny.

The room grew still, as still as the day before creation.

"Here's the windup," said the announcer, "and the pitch."

In Paradise, the Lord of the Universe tosses a green ball which breaks into a silver ball which breaks into a gold ball, and small plane lands safely at Willow Run and Hal Bishop climbs out, singing for joy. He is too far away to hear the crack of the bat, like a tree falling all alone in the forest. But he hears the distant cheering. Clare starts running and Ben runs after her as they round the bases, past the living and the dead, heading at top speed for home.

David Rosenbloom

ELIJAH NAMED
MANAGER OF SAINTS

Dateline Savannah, GA: April 6, 1984
Augustine Names "Long Gone" Elijah
Manager of Saints
600 Year Contract: To Retain Player Role

Savannah Saints General Manager Gus Augustine
today announced the appointment of veteran Saint "Long Gone"
Elijah as manager for the '84 season. The contract, whose finan-
cial terms were not disclosed, is stated to be "for 600 years, or
until the realization of the City of God, whichever comes first."
Said Gus, "After observing the peerless talents of this man over
the past sixteen centuries, the choice was inevitable." Elijah will
retain the pinch-hitting and relief pitching role he has held for
the Saints over the past millennium, ever since his retirement in
the wake of the massacre at the hands of the Roman Barbarians
at Massada in the defunct Milk and Honey League. Elijah thus
becomes the first active player-manager since Leo "Proportions"
da Vinci, retired in 1756, played eight positions (all but catcher)
for the Latin Lions throughout the Quatrocento years.

I talked with Elj in his spare but cavernous office, suspended
above the diamond of Kingfish Stadium, on a pleasantly warm
Savannah day. Below, the Saints were engaged in the disciplines
of hitting; sharp cracks of the bat punctuated our conversation,
as the Holy Heavies laid into pre-season pitches with dedication.
Elijah, dressed in the familiar Blue-and-Golds with the number
2 visible on his left shoulder, looked trim and fit, and considerably
younger than his 2881 years.

When asked about changes in the line-up for the coming year, Elj replied: "With the exception of moving Bug Lunch (John the Baptist, 3B, BR, TR) back up to the lead-off spot, and switching Angels (Teresa of Avila, 1B, BL, TL) back to the number five slot, the lineup will remain the same." Why the switch? Elj pulled the visor of his cap down over his eyes as the blinding light broke through the white clouds which dotted the Savannah skies, and replied: "As you know, Bug Lunch started off his career in the lead-off spot, and was certainly one of the best in the history of the game. He was moved to the middle position in the sixteen-hundreds, not only to exploit his power down the alley, but also to put Angels, who'd just come up from a sensational rookie season in our Class AAA affiliate (the Spanish Spears in the Inquisitional League), up in front. In those days, and on through the seventeen- and eighteen-hundreds, it was real unnerving for the opposing pitcher to be up against a couple of clairaudient girls right off the bat: Joan "French Fry" of Arc (2B, BR, TR) had come straight out of junior high in Orleans to join the Saints, and established herself right away as a holy terror on the basepaths— as well as one of the greatest sacrifice players in the game. So the other teams seemed to get real rattled, Joan being as fierce a competitor as she is—and not only a girl, but real *small,* too." He chuckled, and spit a stream of carob juice into the pail. "So when Angels showed up, it was irresistible to put both of them up front. Once they got on base, you know, they'd get the Word, and wham—off they'd go. I think, if you check the Big Book, you'll find that once the girls started working the paths together, we led the league in forcing errors by the opposing catcher on throws to second or third, as well as in balks by the opposing pitcher. But nowadays, with the other girls coming into the league, and even some of them running the ball clubs (like that big girl over there in Loisaida, Gertie Stein), in the last couple of hundred years the shock value has worn off. Teresa has shown enormous power these past couple of centuries, especially to the opposite field; she's driven quite a few far into the upper regions both here and on the road. So we thought we'd let her swing away. Bug Lunch is real aggressive up front; and as you know, he never lets the opposing team forget who's coming up next in the order."

Elj chuckled, as well he might. Who on an opposing team

has not trembled in his cleats as Bug Lunch raved, "Make way, make way! One is coming who is greater than all of us, yes, even than Elijah himself!" Surely no team has not feared the Son of God, Jesus "Main Man" Christ, who wields his mighty bat in the number three spot in the order. What can be said about the Main Man that hasn't been said before, from a rookie season so stunning that all seasons prior to it are referred to, simply, as Before Christ. A lifetime .387 hitter, he holds records so awesome that one hears them repeated as a litany: 379 MVP's, 83 consecutive; 176 triple crowns; 1392 Gold Gloves; and the list goes on. Jesus (SS, BR/L, TR) is a compelling presence, and such awesome talent has been met with appreciation rather than with bitter jealousy; nearly to a man, opposing players have few words to say about him that are not superlatives (although occasional fevers sweep the Leagues proclaiming that he doesn't exist at all—a claim which ends on a sorry note when the teams blow into Savannah). Also perpetual is the hopeful delusion that finds expression as weak teams across the Leagues claim the Main Man to be on their own roster—harmless enough until the team in question finds itself playing against the genuine article. As for the man himself, he takes it all in stride. "I said I'd be with them until the end of the world, and here I am," he says, with a smile and a wink. Expect another .400, 40 home run, 40 stolen base season from Christ.

Following Christ in the batting order is the enigmatic center fielder, Gautama "Not Me" Buddha. A power hitter who rarely strikes out (46,914 SO in 3,521,918 at-bats), Buddha has led the league in slugging percentage 2,348 times—nearly once every two-an-a-half seasons. In recent millenia, he has foregone the long ball for strategic hitting, inspiring sportswriter Bill James to create a new statistic: run-producing at-bats, a category which has lead in every season since its inception twenty-one years ago (excluding the '74 season, when Buddha had left the Saints for a ministerial sabbatical). His effect on opposing players is also unusual. Former scribe hurler Gerry "Quick Pitch" Heard, now a front-office man for the Saints, had this to say about facing the Saints' clean-up man: "I just loved to pitch to him," said Quick Pitch. "Somehow the moment became everything: I could see the pitch, the swing, the movement of the fielders all at once, as in a slow-motion tapestry. I even found myself unconcerned about the outcome of the play, as the game seemed transfigured by a perpetual, clockwork beauty. Of course, when I reached down for the resin bag after he'd positioned himself on second or third, the entire universe seemed to be nothing but an endless cycle of pain. He sure could hit." When asked about remarks such as this, "Not Me" gazed at the white sphere cradled in his hand and smiled, but said nothing. "Having him in the on-deck circle behind Christ really does it," said Elj with relish. "I mean, you're going to pitch around Christ to get to *him*?" He chuckled to himself, and shook his head.

In the number five spot, as Elijah had indicated, is firstbase-woman Teresa "Angels" of Avila. An uncanny knack for scoping out the strategy of the situation has landed All-Star berths for Teresa in ten of the past twelve seasons, after several centuries of consistent quality play. Now, moved to the power pocket of the batting order, we'll see if she can deliver the long ball with the same consistency. We asked her about the switch, and she replied, "I do the bidding of my Lord." We pointed out that the decision had probably been made in the front office, between Gus Augustine and Elijah themselves, without the consultation of the Main Man. She laughed, and said "Oh, that! I'll play anywhere they like! After all, it's *how* you play, not *where*." She smiled, yet somehow I felt admonished by this queen of strategy; after all, I'd been a student of the game through her essential writings on infield play ("Interior Castles") and situation strategy ("The Way of Perfection"). An awe-inspiring figure, especially with the aureole of light which emanates from her person.

Sixth in the order is the hard-hitting youngster, the catcher Martin Luther "Dream Man" King (C, BR, TR). In his fourth season last year for the Saints, Marty socked 18 homers and collected 82 ribbies, despite his not having fully recovered from a pre-season injury to his back. "This is the greatest team on God's green earth," he says, "and by God, we'll keep going until we reach the pinnacle of achievement!" An inspiring player, he has some trouble with strikeouts in the Big Leagues; over the past couple of seasons, Saints batting coach Isaiah (the "I Say" kid) has been working with Marty. "He's a driven man," says Isaiah, "and he has inborn talent. Don't be surprised if this youngster leads the Saints to the pennant by his hustle and determination." When asked about his feelings concerning playing against some teams which have razzed the youngster (fans will recall the incident last year at Mobile's Tarheel Stadium when, having doubled off the wall against Lester "Fat Boy" Maddox, King was presented with a porter's jacket at second base), the Dream Man replied, "Some of the teams in this league haven't looked at the clock for a hundred years: it's time they woke up to face reality." He paused, then resumed, his voice resonant: "With Jesus on our team, we cannot fail; and even if I'm knocked out at home plate, they will still have to deal with our half of the inning!" The young backstop will reportedly wear a bulletproof catcher's vest.

Batting seventh is the eccentric left fielder, Bal Shem "Out There" Tov. Deep in transport when I arrived at the stadium, he was unavailable for interview, so let's turn to the statistics: .301 lifetime batting average, .327 last year; the best hit-and-run record on the Saints, and third-best in the league; and, oddly, a league-leading 164 walks (no one else was close: Davey Crockett of the Appalachian Roughnecks was second with 112). He also manages several two-base steals a season—only the second player to repeat such a feat. "He just doesn't seem to be there," said Jim "Blades" Bowie of the Roughnecks, who once pitched from the wind-up with Tov on first, and then again with him on second, in spite of the desperate gesturings of his teammates. "Then, as soon as you are at the top of your wind-up, you remember—but then, if you stop, it's a balk. What the hell—it's worse than facing the heavy guns of the Mexicans."

Just as I was ready to give up on my chances to talk to the Bal Shem, a little guy in a janitor's suit came in. "Do you know where I can find the Bal Shem Tov?" I asked him. He grinned widely and said no. I shrugged my shoulders—and suddenly felt warm. The little guy appeared at my elbow with a little paper cup. "Drink up," he said, "you'll never know when you'll faint." I eagerly complied, and felt immediately cooled off, and the little guy disappeared down the concrete walkway. Then for some reason I sat down, and didn't do anything. I just sat there . . . and then I came to, with no sense of time. It might be an hour later, I thought; all the players would be packed and gone for the day! I raced out—and it was night, a beautiful moonlit night. A gentle breeze fanned tropical trees, and I sat in the stands until the evening wind grew chilly. Images played out of my mind into the inky dark, from centuries of baseball history: the building of the

magnificent stadium in Jerusalem, and its collapse; the travel-
ling teams, from a small village in India to China and then Japan,
and from Golgotha to Rome; the wandering teams of the Middle
Ages, weaving their way through a plague-ridden continent, playing in every town; the dreaded devastation of entire leagues at
the hands of ruthless owners and general managers, driven by
madness to restrict play to Aryans . . . Image after image melted
into the blackness; time seemed to shift through the centuries,
and souls shifted through time, bringing the fundamentals of play
to land after land, across the ages, again and again . . . I gazed
at the night sky, black and penetratingly clear . . . but I never did
get to speak to the Bal Shem, or to his other teammates, due to
my odd waking nap. So here are the remaining stats.

Batting eighth: Mary "Virge" of Nazareth (RF, BR, TR). A
steady, all-around player, with a quiet, patient attitude that
seems to instill the team, especially the younger players, with
confidence. Seeming to melt into the background, her stats reveal
a great impact. Last year: .283, 6 homeruns, 58 ribbies, 24 stolen
bases. Between Virge and French Fry, the Saints have literally
owned the sacrifice statistic in the league for ages: they have, between them, garnered the title an average 9 out of 10 years over
the past three centuries. "She's quiet," says Elj, "determined and
steady—kind of sits in the background. But I think everyone here
knows what she's done in the past—and what she's capable of."

Batting ninth and pitching on opening day: Lao "No Pitch"
Tse. One of the most enduringly successful pitchers in the game,
Lao Tse has maintained a remarkable 1.97 ERA over a millennia
of play (excluding the years from 181 B.C. to 497 A.D., when he
was not pitching for the Saints, or for anyone else—in fact, no one
knows where he was or what he was doing, and, oddly enough,
his absence wasn't noted until he returned to pitch against the
Dung Beetles in the '97 "Molehill" Series). The only Saint who
suffers from a drinking debilitation (although the entire starting
line-up is prone to ministerial sabbaticals, and all but Buddha
and the Dream Man to transports), Lao Tse somehow manages
to steady himself in most cases and keep a handle on the task.
Famous for his disappearing "Cleave to the Female Principle"
pitch ("No one's ever hit it," says Gus Augustine; "in fact, no
one's ever even *seen* it—and I include myself in that one"), "No
Pitch" is fond of building the count to 3-and-2 whenever possi-

Saints' home opener, April 15, 1984, vs. Loisaida Scribes

	1	2	3	4	5	6	7	8	9	R	H	E
Scribes	0	0	0	0	0	0	0	0	0	0	2	2
Saints	0	0	0	0	1	1	2	1		5	10	0

Loisada Scribes

NAME—Offense	Pos	AB	R	H	2B	3B	HR	RBI	S	HP	BB	SO	PD	A	E
1 KAFKA	2B	4	0	0	0	0	0	0	0	0	0	0	2	1	0
2 HEMINGWAY	RF	4	0	1	0	0	0	0	0	0	0	0	5	0	0
3 DICKENS	3B	3	0	0	0	0	0	0	0	0	1	1	1	5	0
4 TOLSTOY	C	3	0	1	0	0	0	0	0	1	0	0	2	1	0
5 AUDEN	1B	3	0	0	0	0	0	0	0	0	1	0	10	0	0
6 DOSTOEVSKY	CF	3	0	0	0	0	0	0	0	0	0	0	1	0	2
7 MELVILLE	LF	3	0	0	0	0	0	0	0	0	0	1	2	0	0
8 FITZGERALD	SS	3	0	0	0	0	0	0	0	0	0	1	1	2	0
9 SHAKESPEARE	P	2	0	0	0	0	0	0	0	0	0	2			
MILTON	PH	0	0	0	0	0	0	0	0	0	1	0			
TWAIN	P	0	0	0	0	0	0	0	0	0	0	0			
Totals		28	0	2	0	0	0	0	0	1	3	5			

NAME—Pitchers		IP	R	ER	H	2B	3B	HR	SO	BB	WP	HB			
SHAKESPEARE	L(0–1)	7.0	4	2	8	1	1	1	1	1	0	0	0	3	0
TWAIN		1.0	1	0	2	0	0	0	0	1	0	0	0	0	0
Totals		8.0	5	2	10	1	1	1	1	2	0	0	24	12	2

Savannah Saints

NAME—Offense	Pos	AB	R	H	2B	3B	HR	RBI	S	HP	BB	SO	PD	A	E
1 THE BAPTIST	3B	2	1	0	0	0	0	1	1	0	1	0	0	2	0
2 JOAN	2B	4	0	1	0	1	0	2	0	0	0	1	0	2	0
3 THE CHRIST	SS	4	1	2	0	0	1	1	0	0	0	0	2	5	0
4 THE BUDDHA	CF	4	0	2	0	0	0	0	0	0	0	0	4	0	0
5 TERESA	1B	3	1	0	0	0	0	0	0	0	1	0	9	1	0
6 KING	C	4	0	1	0	0	0	0	0	0	0	0	6	0	0
7 SHEM TOV	LF	4	1	3	0	0	0	1	0	0	0	0	3	0	0
8 MARY	RF	4	1	1	1	0	0	0	0	0	0	0	2	0	0
9 TSE	P	2	0	0	0	0	0	0	1	0	0	0			
Totals		31	5	10	1	1	1	5	2	0	2	1			

NAME—Pitchers		IP	R	ER	H	2B	3B	HR	SO	BB	WP	HB			
TSE	W(1–0)	9.0	0	0	2	0	0	0	5	3	0	1	1	0	0
Totals		9.0	0	0	2	0	0	0	5	3	0	1	27	10	0

Scribes lineup by David Schiller

ble, and then asking the batter what he'd like to see next. "It unnerves the hell out of them," says Elj; "Maybe that's why he's such a great Saint." His off-speed pitch was purported to be the best in the league, but for reasons unknown to everyone except himself, he has stopped throwing it, and resorted to the creation of a new pitch, known as the "No-Ball"; thus far, he has not used it in play, but has promised to unveil it this year. We asked his catcher, the Dream Man, what it was like. "If I could describe a house that was so high, you couldn't see the height of it; and so deep, you couldn't see its depth; and so wide, you couldn't see its width, I would do so—but no man can—and I, I am a man." Throws left.

The remaining pitching rotation:

Moses "the Lawman": Occasionally wild, a burning heater, unbeatable when he's on. Hot-tempered when dealing with inexperienced teammates (he once smashed the clubhouse chalkboard in frustraton with his inattentive teammates while in the Desert League), he has found the Saints to be a stabilizing influence. A good bet for 15 to 20 wins again this year, though he may require relief. Throws right.

Teilhard "Phenom" de Chardin: A careful, studious pitcher, with pinpoint control; led the Saints in complete games last year with 16. Strong and steady, not as overpowering as the Lawman, nor as erratic as No Pitch; possesses one of the most surprising moves in the game—he picked off 1.5 runners a game last year. Throws right.

John "Reedman" of the Cross: A moody hurler with "the best innate sidearm delivery in the game" according to former teammate Gus Augustine. Can he develop that talent? It remains to be seen. The only hurler with a recent no-hit game (one in '83, and one in '81), he is also lowest in wins-per-year on the staff, and prone to spells of concentration lapse. The highest transport ratio on the team doesn't help—but young catcher Marty King might. What does the Reedman say? "The wind will blow as it will blow . . . " Throws left.

Therese "Zounds" Newman: Another high transport ratio, but in the bullpen this time. "When she's on, the opposition can forget it; she makes them see things they've never seen before.'' Thus spake Zarathustra, the bull power hitter for the Philosophers, after her rookie season. Since then, it's been on again, off again for Therese. But last year, she notched up 31 saves and a strikeout ratio of 1 per 4.1 batters, second best in the division. Off to a hot spring training, she's a good bet to be big trouble for opposing teams in relief. Throws left.

Richard A. Russo

---

from
THE UNKNOWN
STORY OF BASEBALL

I. The Journeys of Basho

Matsuo Kinsaku, born in Japan in 1644, changed his name to Basho and became the first great *haiku* poet. Basho was also an itinerant ballplayer, who earned his keep by putting together pick-up teams of fellow journeymen and playing exhibition games against the local champions. Each fall he retreated to his modest hut in Fukagawa to spend the winter writing; each spring, he looked forward to touring the countryside again in search of new inspiration:

> Spring air,
> scent of plum—
> the Season is upon us.

In his youth, Basho was known primarily as a pitcher with deceptive speed, though he longed to be recognized as an outstanding batsman. "The essence of pitching is *wabi* [humility]," he once said, "for a pitcher is only as good as the defense behind him. But the essence of batting is *sabi* ['contented solitariness']."

Once, after a close game, a Zen student who'd lost a substantial sum betting against Basho's team angrily challenged him to explain how he could reconcile the principles of Buddhism with the practice of baseball. Basho quickly replied,

> A ball
> leaps from a bat—
> hear the sound!

In later years he lost his fastball and had to move to leftfield, until his legs gave out and he retired from the game. It is said that several hundred people came to Edo to watch him play his last game beside the cherry-blossomed groves of the Sensoji temple in Asakusa. The poet hurled a three-hit shutout, doubled in his first two at-bats, and then, after flying out deep to center, laid down a perfect bunt in the final inning to squeeze home the winning run.

The following spring, when asked how he was getting along now that he could no longer play ball, Basho thought for a moment, then replied,

> After a recent rain
> the grass has grown greener
> than ever before.

Despite this outward calm, he missed playing the game. Later that spring he wrote one of his most moving poems:

> Old legs—
> still yearning
> for the playing fields of Edo.

In old age, Basho's love of the game was deepened by his retirement from active play. As a spectator, he found baseball the perfect expression of *karumi,* the ideal of detachment he sought in his writing. Each game was an opportunity for the calm contemplation of profoundly-felt truths. A good baseball game, he declared, was like a good poem: its movement light as "a river bubbling over a shallow bed," yet its outcome, in retrospect, "inevitable."

In 1694, as he lay dying, his disciples begged for one last poem. Basho called for rice paper and pen, and wrote these words:

> Autumn grass—
> all that's left
> of batsmen's dreams.

II. The Eye of the Needle

In the winter of 1844, Elias Howe arrived in Cambridge, Massachusetts, at the invitation of his friend, George Fisher. Howe had been wrestling with the idea of a mechanical sewing machine for several years, but his first designs, which imitated the movement of a human arm, had all been failures.

His problem was this: his machine could poke a needle up and down through cloth, but could not pass it all the way through (which would require detaching it from the drive wheel). How, then, could a thread be pulled through the cloth in order to make a stitch?

Fisher knew that Howe had come to an impasse, and offered to provide whatever equipment was needed, as well as food and lodging, so that he could concentrate on the problem without any external distractions. Howe moved in with his friend in October and set up a workshop in the garage. But even under ideal working conditions, he could find no solution, and by the spring of 1845 was ready to give up.

Baseball was the rage in Cambridge that spring, the early variant now remembered as "the Massachusetts game," in which a runner could be retired by "plugging" him (hitting him with a thrown ball). Fisher was a great fan of the local Beaneaters. Seeing that Howe was slowly sinking into despair, he suggested they go see a game, hoping that taking his friend's mind off the problem of the sewing machine for one afternoon would prove refreshing.

"Little John" Manning was throwing for Boston that day, the same Manning whose son Jack would later go 18–5 for the 1876 Bostons in the National Association. Jack aparently inherited his fastball from his father, for on this day, Little John was unhittable. The opposing club could only manage three baserunners against the underhand fireballer, who thrice struck out the side on nine pitches. "They can't touch his fastball," crowed Fisher. "They're swinging right through it." Howe, who'd never seen the game played before, was deeply moved, and even managed to forget his damned machine for a few hours.

Afterwards, Fisher wanted to bring his newly-converted friend around to meet some of the Boston players, but Howe declined. The game had stimulated unexpected memories of his childhood as a farmboy in Spencer, and many a happy afternoon of stoolball [a game in which the ball was thrown at an inverted stool, which the batter had to defend with a stick or his hand]. At the same time, his thoughts had turned back to his sewing machine. In a curious state of mind, nostalgic yet agitated, he returned to his workshop, where he spent several fruitless hours unable to concentrate, then retired early in a deep melancholy. He slept fitfully during most of the night, until finally, near dawn, he sank into a deep slumber, during which he had the following dream.

Manning was again throwing—only this time, he was hurling fastballs at Howe, who sat paralyzed on a three-legged milk stool behind the home plate. A parade of burly little men carrying baseball bats stepped up to the plate to swing at the throws, but try as they might, they could not protect him, for each bat had a hole in the end of it the exact width of a baseball, and Manning's fastball would unerringly find the hole and pass through the bat unimpeded. Howe awoke in a cold sweat, the dull thud of baseballs striking their target echoing in his mind.

That morning, at breakfast, he was relating his nightmare to Fisher when suddenly he pictured the strange baseball bats with holes in their ends and burst out laughing. He'd found the answer to his problem. If his machine could not pull a thread through cloth, it would *push* it through—a feat he'd accomplish by putting the eye of the needle at its point instead of at its base!

Howe finished his design that summer and patented the first sewing machine in September, 1846. After winning a long legal battle with Isaac Singer over patent infringement, he became a wealthy man and, as a devoted fan, donated much time and money to early efforts to organize the game. Howe lived long enough to see a promising young kid named Jack Manning break in with the Red Stockings on the eve of professional baseball.

III. Incident in Vienna

Carl Jung's visit to Vienna to see Sigmund Freud in 1909 proved decisive in severing their once-close relationship. Freud had been touting the younger man as his true successor for some time, a responsibility with which Jung had grown increasingly uncomfortable.

The visit got off to a poor start on the first night, when Jung tried to discuss a dream he'd had in which he kept descending floors of an old house until finally he came upon two ancient human skulls in the deepest basement. He felt that the dream signified levels of the psyche beyond the personal, which would require substantial revision of psychoanalytic theory, but Freud immediately focused on the two skulls and kept asking what wish they represented and whose skulls they were. Finally Jung shouted, "My wife and my sister-in-law!" Freud was satisfied, unaware that his student had purposely told him what he wanted to hear. Jung only grew more depressed. Matters became worse when Freud related a dream of his own, then refused to confide the personal associations that would allow Jung to interpret it.

Both men were in foul moods. Struggling to find some neutral topic of conversation, they turned to baseball, which Freud had introduced to his student two years earlier during their first meeting in March of 1907. (After Freud's death in 1940, Jung acknowledged in a letter to Toni Wolff that whatever their differences, he owed a debt of gratitude to Freud for bringing into his life the two great "sciences" [*wissenschaften*] of the twentieth century: psychoanalysis and baseball.)

At first, they reminisced about the games and players they'd seen during their recent visit to the United States. But the conversation quickly became personal, when Freud boasted to the startled Jung that he could "strike him out on just three pitches." "And what makes you so confident, Herr Professor?" Jung replied sarcastically. Freud smiled and said, "I taught you how to hit."

"I knew then," Jung wrote in his memoirs fifty years later, "that Freud sought to maintain his authority over me at all costs. The end of our relationship was already foreshadowed."

The younger man warned his mentor not to persist in his

foolish boast, or he would be forced to "take him deep." Freud merely turned and entered the parlor, where he drew a bat and ball from an antique wooden cabinet. The two men then walked to a nearby field.

What happened next is not clear. Neither man ever recorded the episode in writing, though both mentioned it to intimate associates. Jung told Toni Wolff that he took Freud's first pitch, in order to "see what he had," then hit a "gargantuan" home run down the leftfield line. Embarrassed at his own need to show the old man up, he then purposely missed the third and final pitch to let Freud save face.

Freud's account of the episode was somewhat different. Anna Freud reported that her father once told her that he'd struck Jung out on three straight pitches, though upon questioning, he'd admitted one of them was a "long foul ball." In Freud's version, he froze Jung with a fastball for a called strike, then had him way out in front of a change-up, which Jung pulled down the line for a foul strike. "A foul home run?" Anna asked. "A foul home run is a strike," her father snapped. "And he missed the third one completely."

What followed next is well-documented. The two men returned home in silence. Freud put the bat and ball away in the cabinet. Then Jung perversely brought up the occult, a subject sure to irritate Freud. Suddenly they heard a creaking sound from the parlor.

"Aha!" shouted Jung. "An example of catalytic exteriorization phenomenon!"

"Bosh," replied Freud.

Jung began to feel a strange burning sensation in his chest, as if his diaphragm were made of red-hot iron. "You are mistaken, Herr Professor," he said.

Just then there was a loud report, like a pistol shot. Both men ran to the parlor. Freud opened the cabinet and they peered inside.

Freud's bat had shattered into a dozen pieces.

Frank Londy

    Enthusiastic TV announcers so often comment on long, long home runs "that ball was hit so well-hit, it would have gone out of any park except Yellowstone."

    With that thought in mind I thought you might be amused with the enclosed photos taken by my wife. As far as I know the only photos of someone hitting a baseball out of America's largest park (at least in the "lower '48").

Thom Ross

LAST STANDS

eddie and i took our
gloves to montana and
played catch beneath
custer hill.
the marble markers
on the ridge above us
had names on them:
cooke
custer
yates
reilly.

in the fading light
of the day and our imagination
it could have been
yankee stadium
and the names in marble would have been:
ruth
gehrig
dimaggio
mantle.

Thom Ross

CUSTER'S LAST STAND
SEEN AS A BASEBALL GAME

Lt. Col. G. A. Custer

Gall

      I am writing this whole game up as a baseball novel. The end has Crazy Horse striking-out the last 5 batters in relief. Seen in actual terms the game is basically historically accurate. It will be illustrated, by me, with pen and ink drawings of the cavalry men and indians dressed as if for war yet carrying bats and gloves in place of clubs and rifles, baseballs instead of bullets.

7TH CAVALRY
(UNITED STATES ARMY LEAGUE)

	AB	H	R	RBI
Reno lf	1	0	0	0
Benteen lf	3	2	0	0
Keough ss	4	1	0	0
Calhoun cf	4	1	1	0
Cooke c	3	1	0	1
Smith 3b	4	0	0	0
Yates 1b	4	0	0	0
Custer, T. rf	3	0	0	0
V. Reily 2b	3	0	0	0
Custer, G. p	3	1	0	0
	32	6	1	1

SIOUX/CHEYENNE
(NATIVE AMERICAN LEAGUE)

	AB	H	R	RBI
Low Dog rf	6	4	2	3
Crow King 3b	6	2	2	1
Gall 1b*	5	3	3	5
Two Moon c	5	2	2	2
Spotted Eagle cf	4	2	1	0
Rain-in-the-Face ss	4	3	2	1
Lame White Man lf	3	0	1	0
Hump 2b	5	1	1	0
Sitting Bull p	4	1	1	2
Crazy Horse p	1	1	1	2
	43	19	16	16

7th Cavalry	100 000 000	1 6 1**
Nat. Americans	101 033 35X	16 19 0

E–Custer, T.   2B-Calhoun, Cooke, Keough, Rain-in-the-Face, Gall, Sitting Bull, Low Dog, Two Moon, Crazy Horse   3B–Crow King   HR-Gall 2, Two Moon, Double Plays-7th Cav. 1   Nat. Americans 1   Left on Base–7th Cav. 5, Nat. Amer. 9

**Gall hits his first of 2 HRS
Little Big Horn River
June 15, 1876**

	IP	H	R	ER	BB	SO
7th Cavalry						
Custer, G. (L)	8	19	16	13	4	5
Nat. Amer.						
Sitting Bull (W)	7	6	1	1	1	7
Crazy Horse	2	0	0	0	0	5

Time–2:45   Attendance–15,683

---

*Gall, the Hunkpapa warrior, hit 2 tremendous home runs into the upper deck of the stadium into a section used exclusively for the witnessing of the Sun Dance. He was a great first-baseman who always played in front of the bag, runner or no runner on. His ham was wrapped in ermine skins and he wore a single feather, standing straight up in his hair.

**The error was Tom Custer misjudging a line-drive off the bat of Crow King.

Thom Ross

BIG SIX

Christy Mathewson stepped out of the centerfield clubhouse
onto the Polo Fields;
emerging in his long linen duster,
smiling and throwing the fadeaway for the
New York GIANTS for sixteen years, (1900–1916);
he finally walked out of baseball and into
the 20th Century,
France,
and mustard gas.

He returned home a sick man
and as the World Series opened in
Pittsburgh, 1925
his lungs burst at last;
Big Six was 45.

July 24, 1986
Jackson, Wyoming

Thom Ross

Enclosed find recent cut-out of NY Giant great, Christy Mathewson, "Big 6".

And all this time you thought he was *dead*!!

Not so, he's "bringin' the heat" live in the Northern Rockies. He struck me out on what I thought was a bad call, low and away. Regardless, he was clocked in the low 90's!!

Thom Ross

HOMAGE TO ROGER MARIS

My friend and second baseman, Frank, has a push-button phone. On the lower left is a push-button with an asterisk. We keep pushing it trying to get thru to Roger Maris but the line is always busy—have you gotten thru yet? and, if so, how is Roger doing? Tell him we're sorry and we hope there is no asterisk in heaven, or right-field, wherever he is.

Jim Hydock

DOCTOR K

The Mets were in town, playing the Giants in homage to Franz Kline. He had grown up in Wilkes-Barre, Pennsylvania, painting brown and green landscapes of coal mines and aging trains chugging over spindly bridges. As a child, his toys were the black cinders along the railroad tracks, and he would come home after dark, covered in dust. He died just past mid-century, leaving paintings of the pearl grey sky seen through the geometry of black trestles.

We had to park on a gravel plateau high outside the concrete stadium, then stream like refugees through the dust to the stadium gates. In their seats the fans chattered nervously, anxious for the first pitch of Doctor K. A black woman, the color of hot fudge, dressed in a white jumpsuit and a Giants cap leaned over to me and whispered, "He is ruthless. There is no need to give him a name." I nodded and stared at the lines on my blank scorecard.

The Giants got to him early, racking him for nine screaming liners, and by the fifth inning he was gone. As he walked off the field the crowd stood on their seats and jeered like a successful junta. In the locker room Doctor K stripped his uniform in a rage. Leaning his thin black body against the steamy white tile of the shower room, he conjured his revenge. "I am the consensus," he seethed, "I am the program. I am the goddamn border patrol."

John Oliver Simon

STELAE

for Richard Grossinger and Bill James

There are stelae from Palenque
that are nothing but names and numbers,
range factor, ERA and triples
for Hunahpú and Hunahpú
who played the sacred game back when
you had to claw for every run
not like today.   The losing manager
got disembowelled on the mound
by the knife of the morning star.

I grow older, hombres, or the children
striding to the plate grow young.
At 41 I played in Xalatlaco,
place-name meaning "sandy ballcourt."
The Zapotec zurdo decked me.
¿Cómo se dice beanball en español?
"¡Así que es pendejo!"
And then for once in my mortal
middle-infielder's vagabond career
I got good wood on the pelota,
it sailed toward the ring of the sun,
reached the ancient wall on one hop.

Hunahpú and Hunahpú played ball
against the gods.   They lost.
They got their heads cut off

and turned them into baseballs on a tree.
A girl ate them.   She had babies:
Hunahpú and Hunahpú.

They finished second two years running,
smoked the candles of the underworld,
came back to challenge in the playoffs.
They used a mosquito in center field
to steal signs.   They stole them blind.
They took the first strike, they went
with the pitch.   They had the long ball.
They sacrificed, they threw the split-finger.
You remember the sequence from Game Six.

The Mayans carved the standings
into limestone.   Learn to interpret
the statistics of heaven,
these cyclic fractals of the endless game.

John Oliver Simon

THE GAME

Inside my heart the page of pentacles
unwinds and deals. The stars that thread the ball
break on the inside corner of the years.

He kicks and fires. I can see his horns.
The airless tarot of the stats reveals
my face must be his own behind the change
which floats along the sudden wind of time.

I swing and get a piece of it. I run
through death and shadow hoping for a bad
hop, a quirk of shortstops in the flow
something to eat that's weaker than myself
a secret path of lime to lead me back
to where my boy-size monster in the heart
roars for October 1st at Ebbets Field
like falling out and into love again
and sliding towards the mystery of home.

Tom Clark

Though it remains a great pleasure to roll the names
and numbers around in what's left of
one's brain, that abandoned bowling alley lane down
which a compacted garbage ball of trivia always thunders
endlessly toward the rooted in concrete steel ninepins
of the facts of life and then bounces and slithers off into
the gutter uselessly, yet not without having diverted one
however briefly etc., still I'm having a harder and harder
   time every
spring connecting the nominative and statistical reality of
the players to these spoiled jockstrap boys from colleges with
a credit card between their teeth when they show up in florida
or arizona with a stockprofile in place of the old dizzy dean
   dream

Steven Goldleaf

THE WAR AGAINST BABE RUTH

The elegant Japanese general listens to his infantry:
"Fukababuroosoo!" Not yet, he murmurs. Meanwhile,
the cancerous Babe lounges, latent, in New York,
all tangerine cravat. Imperial troops still take
his name in vain in Pacific training camps, screaming,
"Fuck BabuRoosoo!" their elocution still imperfect.
The Babe finally breaks 80 on the links,
rasps orders for drinks all around. Why can't
he drink a whole pitcher anymore, ice, fruit, and all?

The troops are losing
an island a month, but their pronunciation
is improving: "Fuck Babe Roos!"
Only the final phoneme
eludes them as they retreat,
island-hopping.
The war ends too soon.

The week of surrender,
the Babe learns why his cravats all fit loose.
He clutches lab reports, tries to read them.
He can no more pronounce the words
than he can swallow.

Three years, he lingers,
until some crazy Jap on an out-island finally
learns to lisp.

Bobby Byrd

PARENTHETICAL STATEMENT FOR THE SEVENTH GAME, 1985 WORLD SERIES

(There is very little poetry.
The breaks fall at the doorstep of George Brett.
Eleven to zip. Whitey gets thrown out.
But not before he brings in Joaquin
to throw gasoline on the fire.
Meanwhile Stoic John has a bleeding hand.
I have a bleeding heart.
Outside the moon is full.
It used to be a harvest moon.
Or maybe an Apache moon.
On television it is a silver dollar.)

Bobby Byrd

A POEM FOR THE 1985 SEASON
OF DOUBLE A BALL,
TEXAS LEAGUE STYLE

Last night I saw Mike Cuellar
Cy Young Award Winner
1969
the year the Baltimore Orioles
won 109 games but got destroyed in the World Series
one game to four
by Tom Terrific and the Miracle Mets.

That was sixteen years ago.

I told my little boy Andy to get Mike's autograph.
"He was one of the best," I told him.

These days Mike is the pitching coach for the El Paso
   Diablos.
His face is brown leather, worn from the sun.
He's a little bit chubby and out of shape.
He must be my age.
At least.
Not an old man, but middle-aged.
And if he's like me, sometimes at night
he lies in bed and thinks about this living flesh
becoming dead and nameless.

So I watched him.

All night long he looked up into the stands
smiling and nodding.
He must have had a special woman up there
waiting for him.
I kept turning around to find her.
I couldn't,
but I could tell from the look on Mike's face
that both of them wanted the game to end.
And when it did
young Juan Nieves had shut out the Jackson Mets
on five hits,
striking out seven.
It was the first shutout at Dudley Dome all year.
Mike Cuellar says Nieves has a good chance
to be one of the good ones in the majors.

"Next year or the year after,
sheet yea!"

After the game everybody crowded around
the handsome young Juan Nieves,
wanting to shake his hand, give him a dollar bill.
All the old Mexican women love him.
They don't care if he is Puerto Rican.
He speaks their language.
"Way to go, Juanito!" they screamed at him.
Mike Cuellar had disappeared.

Bobby Byrd

THE BASEBALL PLAYERS WAIT

in the Dudley Dome
the El Paso Diablos against the Midland Angels
the irony of Double A Ball
an imaginary life
where the grass is really green
really grass
under the lights
where the score is tied 2 to 2
sixth inning
Saturday night
the streets of the city full with drunks
old men and women full with memories
young lovers going to the movies
romancing under the stars

where a boy is sixteen years old
dreaming of his girl's panties
she is being coy
remembering how it was the first time
it was not good
but the boy is insistent
school is out and he is near
to being a man
inside his father's Buick parked
in the little bit of starlight
somewhere in this same desert

where

at the baseball game
there are no stars in the sky
because the lights are on

oh the baseball players
wait
their chance
                    in places in-
between
the expanses of grass
where the dirt is smooth

they wait
and their waiting lets me dream
dream about the boy and girl

she relents says
yes I love you
but thinks to herself
it will be over soon
it will be done with
so that she is surprised
when she becomes happy and glad
the memory of her night
being her naked feet
pressed hard against
the soft material
of the top of the car

so I can forget them to watch the game
the ball
going back and forth
a piece of history unfolding
like the breath of a man
any man
            like myself
breathing

the players still wait
the score is still tied
Glenn Braggs is at bat
two men on base
the players jerk at their pants and shirts
they adjust their hats
they kick at the dirt
they stretch and grab their balls
talking sometimes one to the other
a necessary ritual
to keep the world aright
inside and outside
the chalk marks
the lights
that later will be out
to remember the stars.

June 1985

Bobby Byrd

HAPPY HOUR AT
DUDLEY DOME, 1985

What could be better on a Spring night in El Paso, Texas than watching a baseball game, talking with good friends, and drinking cheap beer? Nothing could! At least, that's what two friends and I thought, all of us bordering on being complete baseball nuts with a taste for beer. So we decided to try out El Paso Diablo's owner Jim Paul's newest idea—Friday Night 5:30 Happy Hour at the Dudley Dome featuring the Diablos against the Beaumont Golden Gators. Real-Live Bush League Ball. It sure sounded like a good way to wind down a week.

I looked forward to the game all week. On Thursday night the paper said that young Juan Nieves, the Milwaukee Brewers' hot pitching prospect from Puerto Rico would be on the mound for the Diablos. I had already seen their other star of the future, centerfielder Glenn Braggs, plow a ball over the leftfield fence with two men on in a tie game. He did what he was supposed to do, and I was duly impressed. Then, after circling the bases, this young man, who will probably be making hundreds of thousands of dollars after a few years in the majors, took the Diablo homerun stroll so that the admiring fans could stuff dollar bills into his baseball cap and shake his hand. That way when he's up there on television circling the bases during the World Series some old woman will talk about how she even put two dollars into that man's hat and how he said Thank you, Mamn, just like any other nice kid. Double A baseball, especially in El Paso, sure is a lot different from the majors.

There are also a bunch of other young players on the Diablos with chances for the future that make this year's club exciting—

Billy Joe Robideaux, Joey Meyer, Juan Castillo. To make things even better for that Friday night, a friend gave us box seat tickets only two rows behind the Diablo dugout. The added incentive of beer for 25 cents a glass was just icing on the cake.

Then, on Friday afternoon, El Paso weather took a strange hard turn to the worse. Huge black clouds rolled into town, pushed by a bitter cold wind. My wife told me I was a fool to go to the game. It was going to rain for sure. Of course, I didn't listen—it was Spring and this was one of the first games of the young season when everything is full of promises. Some of these guys might be called up to dreaded Vancouver in the Pacific Coast League before summer got good and hot. It was not a game to pass up, no matter how cold it got, and everybody knows it doesn't rain in El Paso in the spring. I put on my jacket, grabbed my binoculars, and told my wife the cheap beer would keep us warm. She looked at me like I was crazy. She wouldn't talk to me. I headed for the Dome.

Sure enough, my buddies met me at the ballpark. Fred looked a little hesitant, but since we were there, he sure wasn't going to be a chicken and go home. The wind blew, and the clouds were rolling across the top of the Franklin Mountains. They looked like snow clouds, but surely it couldn't snow—it was April 27th. We huddled up behind the dugout, drinking beer and watching Nieves finish his warmups. Fred kept moaning, saying he thought maybe we should go home. I told him that the mountains looked beautiful with the thick clouds hooked on their peaks. He shook his head thinking, like my wife, that I was a fool.

But at least I was not the only fool there—1,415 fans had showed up to drink the beer and endure the cold wind. Most of them were guys, and the only women at the game were all decked out in pretty clothes. They seemed on the first leg of a long night of partying that just happened to start at a basegall game drinking 25 cent beer. Everybody was in a good mood, laughing and talking and chugging at the beer. Cold or no cold, wind or no wind, it looked like it was going to be a fun evening. The three of us joined in, shivering and sipping at our beers.

The Dudley Dome, no matter what else was to happen, would make the game interesting. It's real name is Dudley Field named for some ghost out of El Paso's history. The place is a matchbox with real grass. I don't know how in the hell it got its nickname—

"the Dome"—because it surely doesn't have any kind of covering, except the usually hot desert sky. I guess everybody just enjoys the bush-league irony of the title. It's your basic, old-fashioned ballpark shoved into the corner of a parking lot, a tiny place, and the high walls don't make up for much. Pop-fly home runs are as common as hard hit singles off the walls in the power alleys. The Dome has the record for the most runs scored in a professional game, something like 31 to 25 in a game just last year. "The wind was blowing out," is what all the sports writers said, somewhat awestruck. True baseball aficionados thought it shameful. The city fathers were somehow proud, even though the Diablos lost the game. Needless to say, the place is hated by players around the league. It's despised and cursed by all pitchers, whether friend or foe. An E.R.A. of 4.00 inside the Dome is considered big league material.

Just as the game started, four young guys, all about 21 or 22, wandered down to their seats which were in the first row right in front of us. Each of them balanced four beers perched on top of concession boxes. They were cheering before they sat down. One of them, a big guy with curly hair, was sucking on his second beer when the first guy up hit a fly ball to center field. It was the first try of the evening for the flashy Braggs who stood nonchalantly waiting for the ball. The wind, though, took control and pushed the ball down and off to Bragg's left. At the last second he lunged for it at his shoelaces, but it spit off the side of the glove, and the young phenom was chasing the ball as it rolled across the grass. The four guys starting hooting. Nieves stared out to his centerfielder in disbelief. "Error" flashed on the scoreboard. Braggs shook his head in embarrassment and strolled back to his position.

The big guy in front of us was slugging down his third beer and pounding his partner on his back. "Ain't this fun?" he screamed in his ear. Then, with his unfinished beer in hand, he headed for the concession stand for another box of beer. Nieves finished out the inning strong. My friends and I huddled up in the cold and talked baseball, every once in a while calculating the Beer Consumption Rate (BCR) of the guys in front of us. Fred still thought the smart thing would be to go home. I joked with him and called him a sissy, but I could see that, if the weather got much worse, Chuck might start tilting his way. I surely didn't want to be out in this bad weather all by myself.

But, lucky for Jim Paul and the rest of us who love baseball, Nieves seemed pretty hot. In fact, he struck out the side in the second inning. That sort of warmed everybody up. Ed Vosberg, the pitcher for the Gators was doing pretty well himself. Through the second inning, nobody had a hit. The line at the beer stand got longer between innings. The fans figured if the players could play, then by gosh they could watch the game, at least as long as the beer held out. And that's what I told Fred. We just needed some exercise to warm up. The best way to do that was to go get more beer. That's what I did. Chuck went for hot dogs. Fred went for nachos.

In the third inning, Beaumont got a run on a couple of cheap hits. The Diablos came back and tied the score. Meanwhile, the BCR for our neighbors in front of us, as well as for 1,413 fans (myself included, but Fred and Chuck, being wiser than myself and most other people there, started to straddle the wagon) continued to race ahead. In fact, there were fewer and fewer fans in their seats and more and more standing in line either at the beer stand or wobbling down the concrete corridors toward the rest rooms. The four guys in front of us were the epitome of what was going on in the rest of the stadium. They were having a ball, hooting and hollering at the players and the umpire and at Dick Poe's Diamond Girls who every once in a while would brave the cold wind and dance on top of one of the dugouts.

To them drinking was the game, and the baseball game was simply a reason to buy beer for 25 cents a glass. The curly-headed big guy was well in the lead in their particular competition. His BCR was much more impressive than Bragg's batting average or Nieves' E.R.A. By the fourth inning he had consumed four boxes of beer. That seemed to be his pace—four beer an inning or six outs for a ratio of 2-to-3. Even Chuck, a real baseball statistician, was impressed by the man's state. His buddies tried to keep pace, but they couldn't. You could see in their eyes that they admired him. When he cheered, they cheered. When he drank, they drank. When he stood up and booed the umpire, they stood up and booed him too. He was the Champ!

The weather continued to make everybody uncomfortable, and in the fifth inning it even began to threaten the game. That's when the black clouds relinquished their patience with baseball and the rains started. It was a hard steady rain, the kind that, when I am warm and cozy at home, I like because I know it is feeding the desert and my lawn good sweet water. But at the domeless Dudley Dome rain is a different matter. Like most everybody else, we headed for the grandstand and the protective covering of its roof. Some of the fans figured 25 cent beer and a baseball game in the rain couldn't measure up to the warm insides of a bar or their living room, and they headed for their cars. It passed our minds too, but we had become too interested in the game. We got another box of beers and packed ourselves in to the grandstand seats with the rest of the baseball fans and/or beer drinkers. We were going to stick it out.

Then there were our four friends, the happy-go-lucky musketeers. The rain didn't phase them a bit. Their BCR continued on its steady course, and now that we were gone, they could stand up and continue their fun without having to worry about the middle-aged men behind them.

For the Diablos, things were getting tough. As the rain poured down and the players surely shivered out there in the field, Beaumont pushed two runs across in the fifth against Nieves, the big hit being a double off the left field wall. He was probably the most miserable guy out there, pitching in the cold as the rain soaked into his uniform. He was probably hoping that the rains would dump enough water on the field to call the game before the last out in the fifth inning, thereby ending it without an official decision against his good name. More than that, he was probably wishing he was back in warm Puerto Rico. This was surely not the hot Southwestern desert he had heard about. I felt sorry for him as I sipped at my beer under the roof of the grandstand. Here was this poor 20-year-old kid from Puerto Rico pitching his heart out in a park that gives up home runs like a school teacher gives grades. He had struck out seven and the other team had only three runs, two of which were as cheap as Jim Paul's Friday night beer. I mean, he had done a damn good job.

But by this time I was just as interested in seeing how the four musketeers would make out as the rains continued. Could they maintain their heroic BCR in the rain and be happy at the same time? They did just that and more. They stood there bravely —although a little wobbly—in the rain and cheered. When Nieves gamely killed Beaumont's rally, they took personal credit for a job well done, bowing to the grandstand and waving.

Then the Diamond Girls climbed onto the top of the dugout, I couldn't tell what they were most concerned about—the rain or the four drunks who were giggling and gawking at their cold legs. But they too persevered. The loudspeaker blared out a loud rock and roll number, and the girls danced. So did the musketeers. They danced like they were all alone with the girls on a dark disco floor. The big-guy with the curly hair was the best. He danced, he cheered, and he applauded. He loved it, and the more he worked out, the more the girls loosened up. His friends, watching how their buddy did so well, did the same thing. The girls smiled and laughed at them, but especially at the big guy. He blew them kisses and he pounded his friends on the back. The Diablos might be losing, but he figured he was winning the game all by himself.

The rains continued, and Vosberg continued to cut the Diablos down, one-two-three with a single thrown in here and there. Nieves also kept the lid on Beaumont. He was really pitching well. In the seventh, the announcer announced "last call" for 25 cent beer. The grandstand emptied out, rain or no rain, to stand in the long line that curled all around the roots of the stadium.

Nieves was missing when the Diablos came out in the eighth. Bevington, the Diablos manager had taken him out. He had pitched well, but not well enough. He could only hope that the Diablos would rally and at least he would not lose the game. Norton came on as the reliever and got three outs.

The rain had stopped.

Then, in the bottom of the eighth, the Diablos tried to put together a rally. They got two men on with no outs. Gator manager Bobby Tolan, who used to play left field for Cincinnati's Big Red Machine back in the glory years of the early seventies, strolled out to the mound to talk to his pitcher. Tolan left Vosberg in, and Dave Klipstein took the count to three-and-two. Vosberg pitched, the ball bounced in front of the plate, but that didn't matter because Klipstein swung, striking out on a pitch that would have loaded the bases. He was too cold and hungry. It had been that kind of night for the Diablos. Tolan decided to go with his reliever. Vosberg walked off. Being good baseball fans, Chuck, Fred, and I cheered him. He had pitched a hell of a game, giving up only one run and only one extra base hit, a double, among six other puny singles. That is a masterpiece in the Dome.

While the Gator reliever was warming up, I looked over to see what the musketeers were doing during this most exciting part of the game.

Nothing. They had left. Vamoosed.

They had stayed during the cold. They had braved the miserable wind. They had laughed at Braggs when he dropped the ball. They had forgave him and cheered when he came to bat. They had cheered Nieves through the fifth when the rains had let loose. They had maintained a steady BCR. They had entertained the rest of us. And, unlike the rest of us, they had not fled to the dry warmth of the grandstand. In fact, they had gotten soaked and probably would have come down with pneumonia if the beer hadn't been coursing thru their veins. Truly, they had not faltered. But pulling the plug on the 25 cent beer was too much. It was moral outrage. They would not allow this last bit of sabotage. It was the last straw. They probably promised themselves never to come back to the Dome, at least never until Jim Paul started selling beer for 25 cents again. They disappeared into the parking lot.

The rest of the game provided little excitement for Diablo fans. To add insult to injury, the Beaumont reliever came in for Vosberg and did his job, getting the next two outs as if the Diablos were weak sisters. Then, in the ninth, continuing the recent tradition of the Diablo bullpen, Norton took the suspense out of the game, giving up five runs on three hits and two walks. The Diablos were suddenly seven runs behind. Then in the bottom of the ninth, the Beaumont reliever again did his job. The Diablo honchos—Robideaux, Braggs, and Meyer—took their turns at the plate, but they looked foolish swinging away for the fence in the cold night air. They came up with nothing. It was over.

My friends and I had stuck it out to the end. We are true baseball fans. We looked around the park and were happy to see that there were others like us. It is real interesting to us just to see players, win or lose, walk off the field after a game. Unlike football or basketball players, these guys just look like average people—athletes for sure, but still, normal people—who happen to get money for playing a game. Watching them play, we had looked at the clouds and shivered, we had relaxed, we had laughed, we had thought about leaving, we had drank beer, we had run for the grandstands when the rains came, cramming ourselves into the few seats with the rest of the fans, and, in the last few innings, we had made plans for coming back again. San Antonio would be in town soon, and they have a couple of guys who might be playing for the L.A. Dodgers next year. And anybody knows the Dodgers need help. Ask Fernando Valenzuela. And when you do, ask him about the Dudley Dome. He pitched a few games here too.

Jerry Klinkowitz

PLAYING THE GAME AT WRIGLEY FIELD

Wrigley Field, home of the Chicago Cubs since 1916, is probably the most celebrated ball park among current accounts of the game.

Only three other stadiums from its pre-World War I era still exist—Briggs in Detroit, Fenway in Boston, and Comiskey on Chicago's south side—and among them it is by far the most beautiful.

Several major league facilities have been built and already torn down in its wake, notably Metropolitan Stadium outside Minneapolis (1961–1982), and it is shocking to note that the next oldest field in the league after Wrigley is the Giants' Candlestick Park, whose current 27th season promises to be its last.

But age and beauty are only part of its appeal. True, the stands are nestled closely in a residential neighborhood, with apartment windows overlooking left and right field. A bar called Murphy's Bleachers sits in the shadow of the scoreboard, where in many larger parks it would be part of the bleachers themselves. And, of course, there are the well-sung features of ivy-covered brick walls, plenty of seats down close to the action and no lights.

The long-debated lighting question has its roots in aesthetics. Although lights were ordered and fixtures half-installed by 1942, owner P. K. Wrigley blanched at seeing his lovely ballpark look like a railroad yard, and so he pulled the equipment down and gave it to the Navy for the war effort.

All these factors contribute to the stadium's fame, but none of them would bear the currency they do without one additional factor—the mass exposure and publicity of Wrigley Field on daily cable broadcasts by WGN-TV.

Most major league baseball teams are on local television or a pay-TV sports channel, limiting their regular audience to a few hundred thousand at best. All 26 clubs rotate on NBC's Saturday Game of the Week, and although the viewership averages 4 million, the chances of seeing any one ballpark more than once a month are slim.

Virtually all the Cubs' games appear on WGN cable, meaning 28 million viewers can catch the team on a daily basis.

The vines, brick walls and ancient hand-operated scoreboard are seen more often than any other features in baseball, making Wrigley Field as familiar as the game itself.

Because the Cubs often host the only day game in the major leagues, newspapers find it easiest to run an early-arriving wire photo of action from their park. In the imagination of most Americans, this is where baseball is played.

Nor is it just the game that's telecast. Thanks to the effectively self-serving hoopla of the Cubs' broadcast team, viewers can expect predictable yet amusing antics from a regular commedia dell'arte troupe of characters, from buffoonish Harry Caray through straight-man Steve Stone to the silent yet oft-remarked presence of director Arne Harris in the truck.

Arne plays the horses, losing most of the time; Steve likes to asphyxiate Harry with his overpowering cigars; and Harry himself keeps fresh his reputation as the Mayor of Rush Street by sloshing down Budweisers from the third inning on. The two announcers pass the time by spelling players' names backwards, doting on ball girl Marla Collins, and teasing Arne about his hopeless nags. Their routine has all the familiarity and homeyness of situation comedy, and contributes to the sense viewers have of dropping by the park each day.

The real achievement of Wrigley Field baseball, however, is that nothing is faked. Fans can purchase a ticket, see a game and find the ambience much the same as pictured on TV. The 11 camera angles (more than for even the World Series on network) are, with the exception of the recently added position atop the scoreboard, among the most popular perspectives from which to view the game. And because of Wrigley's cozy dimensions, just about every shot includes the closeup presence of fans. Frame Leon Durham in the batter's box and you automatically have a dozen faces in the stands looking over his shoulder. Tune in for a week and you'll begin to recognize the same people, just as if you're sitting among season ticket holders yourself. Plus with Harry Caray slurping beer at you, it's almost like being at the park.

Wrangle a press pass and get down on the field, and you'll find not one bit of the mythology changes, even up close. The late morning's cool and quiet sits easily among the empty stands, with today's starting pitcher taking some extra batting practice as the only distraction. After this the "extras" will drift in for their swings—Davey Lopes, Jerry Mumphrey, Manny Trillo and the other past-their-prime veterans who serve as pinch-hitters.

With Don Zimmer batting fungoes to the infield, and Billy Williams studying hitters from behind the cage, the view is like a highlight film from the Sixties.

With the regular comes the sense of being part of the latest video tape feature. Ryne Sandberg, Durham and the other starters walk past you to hit and seem several inches taller but otherwise just like their image on TV. The sound from countless interviews is there too, as Keith Moreland's oddly high-pitched voice complains to a Louisville Slugger rep about his splintering bats and Jody Davis drawls about taking some bunts. Suddenly it smells like a garbage fire has engulfed the city, and there's Steve Stone with a cigar big enough to be a vaudeville stage prop. He speaks with the same earnest, sing-song tone in which he conducts on-the-air interviews, even though how it's just some personal words exchanged with Giants' coach Bob Lillis about his days teaching Joe Morgan how to play second base.

Steve's in character despite the camera's being off and the gates not yet open. Where's Harry? Like the Cubs' starters, he waits 'till last. Meanwhile there are some members of this commedia troupe to be seen strutting their stuff.

As Ron Cey waddles out for his swings, you head down the line toward the left field corner, where Steve Trout, shagging Cey's liners off the fence, calls "heads up, watch it, buddy" as a hot one rips past you, so you turn to focus on the reportedly zany left hander. He's quiet for a minute as you fiddle with your camera, then at the last moment he warns you "Don't shoot, don't take my picture."

Lowering your camera you see he's in a compromised position, readjusting his pants. "I bet you'd like to sell that shot to the National Inquirer," he says, and you identify yourself not as a pro photographer but as a visitor from the Midwest League.

"Midwest League?" he ponders in great bewilderment, and repeats it. "Midwest League, what's that, a magazine or something?" No, you explain, it's a minor league, the Cubs have a team there in Peoria and you're from Waterloo. "Midwest League?" he asks again, still perplexed. And in the same tone of puzzlement he tells you that he pitched in the Midwest League. He then wanders off, still wondering about it all.

Back to the batting cage, where the Giants are now out to take their swings. Still no sign of Harry Caray, though manager Jim Frey, oddly distant and looking grimly like a condemned man (he has since been replaced), has settled on the bullpen bench, far removed from the action.

You're ready to pack it in and head up to the press dining room for a quick pre-game lunch when the man appears—Harry himself, coming through the field gate and into the Cubs' dugout like an ocean liner into berth, as strangely unreal in person as the greatest celebrity might be. He's cheered like royalty and waves back with the stiff little gesture and frozen smile that distinguish the Queen Mother on parade. Up close he shines like waxed fruit, a Madam Tussaud animation of his public self, perfect in every detail except for his belly which doesn't show on the broadcasts. Here in person you can see him walk through the dugout taking bow-legged rocking steps, the image of a man lugging a 27-inch TV set.

From game time on, the Wrigley Field operation is pure class, from the p.a. announcer, Wayne Messmer, whose voice has the lyric opera quality which makes his singing of the National Anthem a stirring treat, to the immaculate condition of the stands. Afterwards, a visit to the locker rooms completes the picture. The visitors' clubhouse is located at the end of a maze of tunnels and unmarked doors leading up behind the grandstand, across a surprisingly open catwalk above concessions, and into a medium-sized room hardly more glamorous than facilities in Midwest League. The Cubs' quarters, recently enlarged and remodelled, are right behind their dugout and are better furnished, boasting a weight room where Chris Speier (who hasn't played today) works at the pec-deck with the same look of concentration as when edging in for a bunt.

At the lockers themselves the myth of celebrity finally breaks down. There's a lot more midriff fat on some pitchers than you'd imagine, and it's a shock to see an outfielder chain smoking. Wearing jeans and a tee-shirt Ron Cey looks no more like a penguin than you or I, and in defeat this suddenly last-place team appears quite human. Bob Dernier speaks softly to a reporter about a broken squeeze play which cost the game, while the rest of the Cubbies are left to themselves. Though no one's drinking, a can of Bud Lite sits atop each locker like a dashboard Jesus, a prayer for better days.

But an hour after the game the Wrigley Field atmosphere still prevails. Murphy's Bleachers is crowded, and behind the right field stands Sheffield Avenue teams with people partying like the old days on St. Louis' Gaslight Square. The elevated trains are making their gametime stops at Addison Street, and while waiting for the local, north and south-bound fans tease each other across the tracks. Get off the 'El' five stops later in the Loop and chances are folks will ask who won. They all know you've been to Wrigley Field—a Renaissance museum of baseball, the Florence of the major leagues—and wish they'd been there, too.

Jerry Klinkowitz

FIVE BAD HANDS,
AND THE WILD MOUSE FOLDS

The Mason City Royals are busing it across the state, and an hour out of Bettendorf, catcher Jim Smith announces that he's finished up his league chart. "Bettendorf!" yells Johnny Mueller before Jim can even begin, "Smells like a catfish in the showers!" "Dubuque!" Joey choruses in, "Cat yuck in the rugs!" One by one they check off the North Central League cities, small burgs of 40,000 folks or so where sometimes there isn't even a Holiday Inn, not that their GM could afford it. The Royals go into each city four times a year, and Jeff has booked them seasonal rates in motels which would otherwise stand empty. And for a good reason. "Oshkosh: big June bugs mashed up in the sheets! Eau Claire: smells like dead stuff in the walls!" Eddie perks up, senses his turn. "Caedar Rapeeds!" he trills in his high Panamanian accent, "La cuckaracha!" Jim Smith shouts for order, claiming they've got it all wrong. He runs down his list of sundry pests and vermin, noting approval and shrugging off complaints ["The zitty waitress is in Davenport, moron"]. But everyone agrees he's saved the best for last. "Green Bay!" he sings out, and the whole bus answers in a single voice, "The wild mouse!"

Their four-game sweep in Bettendorf primes them for the Northern Division, and the luxury of an off-day's travel gets them into Green Bay early enough for some serious poker.

"You gotta lend me five
Just to keep me alive."

Donny the left-fielder is making up a new ditty for each hand, fitting the beat of slapping cards, jingling chips and popping can tops. For a minor league baseball club, the Royals make a good rhythm section when they're playing for blood; it sounds like a bass line behind a nasty whining Mick Jagger song.

"I'd pay you back quick

But my brother got sick,"

and Andy is dealing out another hand. "Garbage," he calls, not his hand but the name of this particular poker round, each dealer calling his pick. Two queens, two deuces. Should he play on a double pair when everybody's drawing three, tossing three, drawing two more?

"How about a ten

till I see you again?"

But he's a long way from borrowing. Nobody's had much good stuff that night, so the pots and losses have been small. The game was better on the bus up from Bettendorf, part of the crazy energy from the ball park riot two nights before. "Game called on account of madness," the paper read. The Royals won on a forfeit called by the ump; the next night the stands were full, hoping for a repeat. Lots of action, but all legal—a dozen home runs between the two teams, tied a league record, score like a football game, 14 to 13, one of the writers said he'd head it "Dodgers miss point after." Plus all sorts of good baseball. Carl's sucker pickoff worked three times; he was right, the runners never learn. Four wins in Bettendorf on top of the game from the Wisky Rapids Kings put them way, way out front, and now when they finish in Green Bay, they'll be looking at a lazy four-game/four-day series in Eau Claire, odds they'll sweep. Oh, oh, Eau Claire. Donny knows a girl up here who'll cook for him all week, so that's six dollars meal money for the poker pot each night. Right now she's across the courtyard watching TV with the players' wives.

Mitch is calling, the crazy bastard. He's the only Green Bay player they'll let in the game, and only because he's shot his credit with his own teammates. Calling the last five hands and the best he's had is a pair of aces. The poor goof. Matt, who took counseling courses when he pitched college ball, says the guy is lonely and that he's only playing cards as a substitute for making friends, which he can't seem to do. So he plays poker like a hyperactive 8-year-old. Maybe he doesn't understand the game.

"Just lend me 20

and I'll show you guys plenty."

For sure he doesn't understand that Donny is singing about

him.

The guys turn in at 2, and within an hour the motel is quiet. But sometime later, Joey hears his roommate get up and head for the john, and a moment later it sounds like a war going on in there. He pushes the door open just in time to see Jim's bat poised over the commode.

The bat slams down with a vengeance, shattering the fixtures and sending shards of porcelain and ceramic tile to the corners of the room. "Take THAT," Jim Smith growls, and swings to position himself for the next blow. But his target is nowhere to be seen. "Close the door, close the lousy DOOR," he yells at Joey, who is calling in Spanish for Ed to come on down and see the fun. It's 4 a.m., lights out was two hours ago, but everyone is waking up as word spreads through the Bay Motel—Jim Smith is clubbing out the wild mouse!

Jim is standing on the toilet, his 40-ounce Louisville Slugger bearing his own stamped signature broken off in his hands. "Joey, Joey, you got a bat up here?" he calls, and Joey laughs back, "No, man, I don't sleep with my bat." "Get me something, come on, get me something," Jim screams again, but now Johnny and Buddy are at the door with Buddy's mosquito spray he'd bought for the murky Bettendorf dugout. "This stuff is industrial strength," he tells the room, "just turn off that fan, close the door and we'll gas the thing through the ventilator." "It's in the can?" Johnny asks, and Jim shouts back, "Yeah man, it's in the shower and I almost had it, but these bats go to pieces, you know."

Buddy's up on the dresser, shaking and spraying his insect repellent through the bathroom vent. Joey starts to cough and sneeze. "Hey, man, you're killing me, turn on the air conditioner." "Forget it, you want to pull it all out?" Buddy protests.

"Listen," Johnny says, "you need a ton of that stuff to even stone it, this is the wild mouse." Every night in Green Bay this season, the mouse has hassled them—chewing gloves, glutting itself in chip dip from the poker table, and one-by-one keeping all of them awake. Of course, they'd like to flatten it, with baseball bats, bug spray or the TV.

"That's it," Johnny announces. "It's gonna want out of that bathroom real bad," he reasons, "so turn out all the lights and get me up here on the dresser with something big." "Smitty's behind," Joey suggests, but Johnny already has the 23-inch vintage black and white TV in his arms. "Bombs over Tokyo," he yells as Buddy slips open the door, the mouse scoots out and the television is dropped from an altitude of seven feet. It hasn't been unplugged.

A sickening roar and phosphorus shower fill the room, condensers sputtering and the main power tubes flashing red and yellow and spitting out sparks. Everyone's yelling and cheering like mad. "Don't touch it, don't touch it," Johnny yells to Joey, "you'll electrocute yourself." He jumps down from the dresser and over to the wall where he unplugs the guttering set.

"Oh boy, oh boy," Jim is repeating. Nobody's hurt, but the room's a mess from the smoldering TV to the sooted-up walls. They kick away the TV shell and there's the charred corpse of a tiny mouse.

"Try mouth to mouth, I think it's still breathing," Johnny says, but nobody's laughing. The team has this entire wing so nobody's heard the bedlam, but tomorrow morning, oh tomorrow morning. "Is Carl's light on?" Jim asks and Joey looks across the court to the coaches' room and it's dark. "I think they're still out," Joey says, but no one knows how to cover this.

"Let's say we were robbed," Joey offers lamely. No one responds. A few sparks from the TV and Buddy jumps. "Easy, man," Johnny cautions, "it holds 2,000 volts, don't touch it."

"I'm calling Jeff," Jim says, and he reaches for the phone. Eight for an outside line, 319 for Mason City, then their GM's home number. "You killed a lousy mouse?" Jeff screeches in his tinny Bronx accent, "a lousy MOUSE?" "Yeah, well you see there's some damage up here, not a lot, but if Carl thinks he has to represent it to you and Mr. Heber . . . " Jeff agrees to put a call into Carl at the desk, he'll get it any minute now that the after-hours bars are closed, and try to take the guys off the hook. The six players in the room will pay all damages from next month's salary. The TV is the worst, maybe the bathroom, but they'll cover it. "And listen, man," Jim pleads, "from now on can you book us in some other place up here?"

"At their pleasure," Jeff assures them, "At their pleasure, I'm sure."

Judy Katz-Levine

CALLING

Falling asleep in the afternoon,
I forget that my father has died.
I anticipate him calling me up,
asking me how my writing is going,
and am I thinking about having children.
Making a joke or two. "Don't worry,
Mom and I will never be lonely."
Then I fall into deeper sleep, he
loses me, traveling in his car, the green
chevrolet, to old baseball fields
which are sweet with rye grass
and lush stadiums, his pals throwing
him the ball—"Give me some pepper, Al."

Bob Stanley

NO SECOND PLACE

For Robin Grossinger

1.

Just as you remember
(was it only last October)
how you jumped up and roared
in the middle of French
when Carter laced the winner
in the fifth, in overtime,

So I remember
no radio, no earphones
when the Yankees closed us out in 'sixty-two

That October afternoon
standing on the knoll where left field ended
we huddled together
eager to dispel the fifth grade rumor
that it was over.
Was it two to one? One-nothing?
Someone said McCovey'd tied it in the eighth.
Expecting one more miracle
we heard the final score.
Yes, the Yankees had done it again.
It was not enough to have taken them to the wire.

You say your father gave up on them that year—
the monotony of winning must have
driven some people mad
like earing caviar for breakfast
(though it's hard to imagine
for one who's waited since that afternoon
25 years to be there again.)

All through my second decade
those Giants bounced balls off walls
and bounced outfielders to other teams
(even now there must be
eleven or twelve, running like elk,
stars in milky-white uniforms
shining against the night,
waiting for some unsatisfied mind
to gather them together once again:
the constellation "Former Giants".

Six years in a row
Second place.
Oh, one remembers
Alan Gallagher and Dick Dietz
(his huge ears & twisted grin)
joining an aging Mays
at the top of the leaders
to win the West in seventy-one

but a division
a mathematical function
is only part of the equation.

When Mays left for Manhattan
the torch moved back
the soul of the Giants returned
(one could say, where it belonged)
and the long drought began.

2.

You could blame the crowds on Finley
or the cold, or the pitching,
or on Lurie's lack of chutzpah;
but they made a run with Alto,
and with Robbie, and with Craig.
They made a run with Laskey
and with Atlee, and with Kruk,
every chase ending
as it ended in the sixties
back when Jim Ray Hart hit fifth
and unknowingly battered homers
into the Hunters Point moisture
while Linzy couldn't get the final out
even then we couldn't quite
get ourselves down the Bayshore
to wait in line to park.

It was warm in Alameda,
Walnut Creek, and San Rafael
and we never had the right amount
of fill in those down parkas.

There was someone from Modesto,
maybe Fresno back in those days
"came to see Mays"
but today he's at the A's
or decided to keep warm
watching Minor League ball.

Yes, it's cold out there
and a little tough to park
but once inside you'll always feel
the magic that springs from that bright green field.

The hope each spring that some young ace
will stun the league with movement and control
flows in us as it flows down the Ohio
lifts our hearts as it pulls New Yorkers,

Bostonians from their dirty February snow.
Our mild Winters and cool Julys
can not alter the balance of a game
that leaves a team alive at the brink.

Though a generation has passed
and new children run beneath Redwoods
(while new grandparents walk behind)
Spring still brings the Giants north
from Arizona to their home beside the bay.
Always unsettling in breezes
both of ocean and opinion,
still they come to play a child's game.

In chemistries that come and go
they try to solve the equation of themselves,
make true a childhood dream of victory.
Mine has grown, faded to an understanding
that win or lose, with black and orange
I choose to stand,
        and this allegiance
           takes no second place.

Bob Stanley

MISSED INDICATORS

Somewhere in that last season
when we knew it was taking you from inside
you called
hoping I'd take you to the game
as you had taken me twenty years before
the night game Mays won off Spahn in sixteen
but by then I was asleep in your arms.

This time it was Gooden
but I was tied up—couldn't make it—
you took the bus—went out there by yourself.

* * *

One April you sent a poem from Paris
some American in Europe had penned.
He missed the crack of the bat
& the dust & the tension & the casual
inattention turning to a roar
all of it untranslatable
along the Champs Elysees.

* * *

The song of life can mirror the peaks
and valleys of the game
we guide each line across a page

a field of vision
as we try to drive
the ball in hopes that it will fall
                              safely

so that we, imagination
                    will go free
                         perhaps advancing

          reaching home

     going to   the game

          with you
     one more time.

David Henderson

SAL MAGLIE

for Richard Grossinger

time grew upon his beard
stubble of days waiting in old mexico
leagues of busrides beyond the trees
a diamond set in itxlan
the score in aztec script
stenciled white foul lines
between tropical coastlands
and mountainous highs
moods for the mind in the bush and cacti
in the beans and the corn
watching the white ball flow upon magnetic lines
to dip towards the center of the rotating sphere
and hit the cowhide squarely
in the middle of earth

somewhere in the leagues to the north
in younger cities of the hemisphere
the nights of the season held as lushly a magical warmth
where the ball would obey the eye of the mind
and the man with the bat would swing at the air

somewhere in the north
in the cities of the eastern leagues
the bearded one would one day play
the motion of his body
plump and fluid following through a *kata*

and the flashing white ball
would float from personal power
to the core of its law

Sal Maglie's stubble beard
sinister atop his white uniform
worn loose and baggy
crouching low to earth
his motion a flurry of flapping fabric
out of which shot the ball
eclipsed in arc by a break in the wrist
stitched ribs fighting atmosphere
suspended in space and driven by force
tilted in a doctrine of signatures
along the axis of home planet
rotating in sympathy and suddenly breaking
to the outer corner of the zone of strikes
shunting force just above a side-arm motion
his curveball was fast and low with a slider's veer
he came to rest in a low crouch
his bearded chin at moxie angle
like a pool player's

his fastball was a beauty of opposites
it rose up and in on a right-handed batter
getting angrily close to the head
(before the game he would always warm them:
you're going down)
left-handed batters hit the dirt equally as well
he could throw so close to the chin
that Sal Maglie became known as "The Barber"

with his mean countenance
one could imagine the gold earring
of a pirate in his ear
but he was a Giant
a Harlem Giant of new york city
Coogan's Bluff once the path of the ancient glacier
was where the Polo Grounds stood

challenging Yankee Stadium which lay
across the Harlem River

old mexico dreams
magical white sphere
hallucinating toadstools
acapulco gold michoacan green
flowing through tropical illusion
zen archer of the floating baseball

ACKNOWLEDGEMENTS AND NOTES

"How I Got My Nickname" from *The Thrill of the Grass* by W. P. Kinsella. Copyright © 1984 by W. P. Kinsella. Reprinted by permission of Viking Penguin.

From *Things Invisible to See* by Nancy Willard. Copyright © 1984 by Nancy Willard. Reprinted by permission of Alfred A. Knopf, Inc.

"Doctor K" appeared first in *Giants Play Well in the Drizzle*, a literary newsletter edited by Martha King. Reprinted in revised form by permission of Jim Hydock.

"Playing the Game at Wrigley Field" appeared first in the *Waterloo* [Iowa] *Courier*, June 15, 1986. Reprinted in revised form by permission of Jerry Klinkowitz.

"Five Bad Hands, and the Wild Mouse Folds" appeared as part of the PEN Syndicated Fiction Project, cosponsored by the National Endowment for the Arts. Reprinted by permission of Jerry Klinkowitz.

"Calling" will appear in Judy Katz-Levine's forthcoming book *Tending*, to be published by Firefly Press, 23 Village St., Somerville, Massachusetts 02143.

Bobby Byrd's new book of poems, *Get Some Fuses for the House: Householder Poems/El Paso, Texas* was published by North Atlantic Books simultaneously with this anthology.

David Henderson's most recent collection of poems, *The Low East*, was published by North Atlantic Books.

Tom Clark's most recent book of poems, *Disordered Ideas*, was published by Black Sparrow Press.

Jerry Klinkowitz is executive director of the Waterloo [Iowa] Indians.